THE STEAM LOCOMOTIVE

THE STEAM LOCOMOTIVE

its form and function

W. A. Tuplin, D.Sc., F.I.Mech.E.

MOONRAKER PRESS

ACKNOWLEDGEMENTS

No book about the steam locomotive in general can be much more than an assembly of pieces of published information and such other as the author could gain from private sources. His task is merely that of making a coherent story out of what appear to be facts.

For the information used in this book the author is specially indebted to the back-numbers of *The Railway Magazine*, *The Locomotive*, *The Engineer* and *Engineering*. Among the books, the outstanding ones are:

Ahrons, E. L. *The British Steam Locomotive*. 1927, The Locomotive Publishing Company. Reprint by Ian Allan, Shepperton

Sinclair, A. *Development of the Locomotive Engine*. 1907, Angus Sinclair Publishing Company. Reprint by The M.I.T. Press, London

Warren, J. G. H. *A Century of Locomotive Building*. 1923, Andrew Reid & Co. Ltd. Reprint by David & Charles, Newton Abbot

The drawing by E. W. Twining is reproduced here as Fig. 2 by permission of *The Railway Magazine*.

Grateful acknowledgement is made to British Railways for most of the photographs of British locomotives depicted in this book and to the builders of the American and European locomotives shown here.

The half-tone illustrations have nearly all been derived from official photographs published by the builders of the locomotives or by the operating railway companies. A great many of the subjects are of the pre-1914 period very near to the zenith of railways.

Illustrations 4a, 4d, 8a and 8b are derived from photographs by F. E. Mackay, a distinguished early specialist in high-definition photography of trains in motion.

The origin of 2d is a photograph given to the writer by Mr W. B. Yeadon and that of 5c similarly came from the late Mr J. M. Dunn who did a great deal of the work required to secure the preservation of No 1054.

The original of 8c was taken by the late Mr H. Gordon Tidey, with permission from Real Photographs Ltd.

Illustration 16b of a Chapelon 4-8-0 is derived from a photograph by M. G. F. Fenino.

The author expresses deep gratitude to all those who provided basic material in published work and otherwise and not least to those who contributed with the proviso 'No names!'

First published in 1974. Second Impression 1980

MOONRAKER PRESS, 26 St Margarets Street, Bradford-on-Avon

SBN 239.00198.2 (paperback 239.00246.6)

Printed and bound in Great Britain at
The Pitman Press, Bath

Contents

List of Illustrations

PREFACE

STEAM on rail came after steam on road. Richard Trevithick who first placed steam on rail in 1804 had previously carried passengers on a steam-driven road vehicle. Twenty-five years later, when the Stephensons' *Rocket* convinced everyone at Rainhill that steam could be commercially viable on rail, one of the other contestants was a steam locomotive similar in style to some of the steam-driven coaches that had been plying on public roads for a few years. Trevithick's locomotive, broadly a colliery pumping engine on wheels, was built in a few months to settle a bet. The *Rocket's* closest competitor, *Sans Pareil*, could be similarly described, but the *Rocket* itself was halfway between a colliery engine and a road-coach engine. It benefited greatly from its novel boiler invented and built in the last few weeks before the Rainhill contest. Each of the two most noteworthy occurrences in the early history of steam on rails thus arose from quick thinking and action to meet what was almost an emergency. During the intervening quarter century, progress had been much less rapid.

The *Rocket* was sound in principle and subsequent development of the steam locomotive was largely in the matter of size to cope with the need to haul heavier loads at higher speeds as the years went by. Provision of the railway network that George Stephenson had visualised was a different matter. It was civil engineering rather than mechanical engineering and there was plenty of experience to work on. In his colliery work, George had had experience of the 'muck-shifting' that characterised much of civil engineering and in developing the extensive network of canals that existed in the 1830s, canal engineers had solved many of the problems to be encountered in laying railways. Canals had to be dead level between locks but as the speed of canal boats was never expected to be high, there was no objection to the sharp curves that were necessary in following a contour line in many places. A railway on the other hand need not be level (although that was always to be preferred) but sharp curves had to be avoided if trains were to run safely at the high speeds of which the steam locomotive had

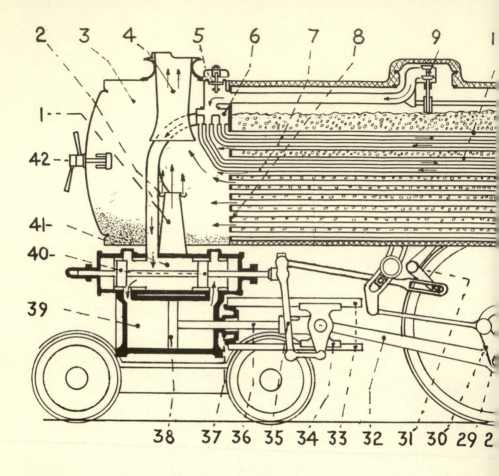

clearly shown itself to be capable. So in turning themselves into railway engineers as distinct from locomotive engineers, the Stephensons had valuable guidance from canal engineering and the extent of the canal network in Great Britain encouraged them to believe that George's vision of a comparably large railway system was not impractical.

What had also to be done, and indeed actually was done for a critical half-century, was to discourage any suggestion that steam power might be profitably employed on the even more extensive British road network. There was cause for some apprehension because commercial use was already being made of the substance, rubber, whose remarkable physical properties were eventually to make it a most effective material for tyres on road wheels. Moreover the pneumatic tyre had already been invented although some 50 years had to elapse before Dunlop re-invented

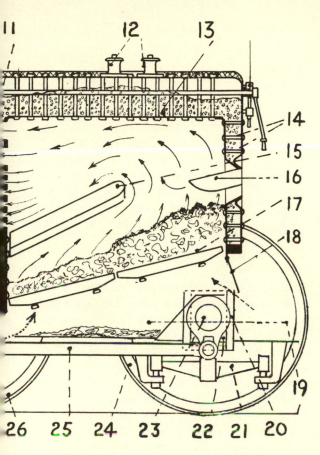

Fig. 1. *Typical steam locomotive*

1. Blast pipe
2. Blower ring
3. Smoke-box
4. Chimney
5. Snifting valve
6. Superheater header
7. Superheater element
8. Tube plate
9. Regulator valve
10. Flues
11. Fire tubes
12. Safety-valve
13. Crown sheet of inner firebox
14. Firebox stays
15. Brick arch
16. Deflector plate in fire-hole
17. Fire bar
18. Ashpan damper
19. Ashpan
20. Hornblock
21. Spring
22. Axlebox
23. Axle
24. Tyre on coupled wheel
25. Coupling rod
26. Tyre on driving wheel
27. Crank boss
28. Crankpin
29. Big end (of connecting rod)
30. Return crank
31. Reversing shaft
32. Connecting rod
33. Slide-bars
34. Crosshead
35. Combination lever
36. Piston rod
37. Gland (grips piston rod)
38. Piston
39. Cylinder
40. Piston-valve heads
41. Steam chest (or Valve chest)
42. Clamp for smokebox door

it and used it first to revolutionise the riding of bicycles. This could hardly have been foreseen in the 1830s but nevertheless repressive legislation was instituted to make sure, and it did so until nearly the end of the nineteenth century. More recently, motors for the multitude have made travel intolerable and telecommunications can soon make much of it superfluous, but for a full century, steam on rail was the major means of land transport of goods and passengers. Although the steam locomotive threw away into the atmosphere about 95 per cent. of the heat in the coal that it burned, it was good enough for well managed railways to pay six per cent. dividends for many years.

HOW IT WORKS

In a book of this kind frequent use must be made of names of components of the steam locomotive and so there is need for early definition and illustration of them. Fig. 1 (p.8) shows the main parts of a typical steam locomotive and the numbered components are named on p. 9.

The origin of power in a steam locomotive is the fire, resting on fire-bars (17) in the firebox whence hot gases pass over the top of the brick arch (15) to enter either the small tubes (11) (about two inches in diameter) or the large tubes (10), (superheater flues about 5 inches in diameter) on their way to the smoke-box (3). From there they are blown out of the chimney (4) by exhaust steam shooting briskly upwards from the blast-pipe (1). The dimensions of the blast-pipe and chimney are adjusted so that steam produced at the rate necessary for the required power output produces enough draught to keep the fire hot enough to maintain that rate.

Water surrounds the inner fire-box and the tubes except inasmuch as its contact with them, strongly heated by hot gases, converts it quickly into bubbles of steam. No one has ever seen exactly what happens and the numerous small circles in Fig. 1 are purely impressionistic. If the pressure of steam in the boiler rises to a predetermined figure (the 'working pressure') one of the safety-valves (12) opens and allows steam to 'blow off' into the open air.

When the engine is working, steam leaves the boiler past the regulator-valve (9) to reach the superheater header (6) where its flow is divided into several paths through superheater elements (7) in which the steam is made hotter by the gases in the flues (10).

From the superheater the steam passes to the (two) steam-chests (41) from which the valve (40) allows it to enter the ends of the cylinder (39) at times when it can usefully push the piston (38). When the steam has done all it can in this respect, the valve has moved to allow it to pass to the blast-pipe (1) without unduly obstructing the return stroke of the piston (38).

Motion of the valve is derived from those of the crosshead (34) and the return-crank (30) by the valve-gear in a proportion determined by the rotational setting given to the reversing shaft (31) by the driver. This decides whether admission of steam to (41) will cause the engine to pull forward or backward, and at what fraction of each stroke of the piston the supply of steam behind it is cut off.

The smoke-box collects a lot of half-burnt coal ('char') drawn off the fire and through the tubes by the draught. To permit of removal of char and of access for tube-cleaning, the smoke-box has a large circular door pulled up tight to its seating by pressure on a handle (42) acting on a screw anchorable to a strong cross-bar.

When the engine runs with regulator closed, the pressure in the pipes between (9) and (41) drops below that of the atmosphere and so the snifting valve (5) falls from the position shown to admit air which then follows the normal steam-path through superheater, cylinders, blast-pipe and chimney to atmosphere.

The smaller wheels under the front end of the engine support a frame or 'bogie' that can swivel horizontally in relation to the main frame and can also move sideways relatively to it against the restoring restraint of springs or of inclination of the sliding surfaces across which weight is placed on the bogie. The sharpest curve that the engine can traverse is defined by the distance between the coupled wheels and by the distance of the leading pair from the bogie. The bogie sets itself to accommodate the curvature of the track. It guides the engine gently into curves.

An accompanying vehicle ('tender') may contain the necessary supplies of fuel and water; otherwise they are carried on the engine itself in which case it is a 'tank engine'.

NOTE ON REFERENCES

A reference, for example (Ref. 6c), means that an illustration of the locomotive appears on Plate 6 and that some dimensions of it are given in Table 1 against Ref. 6c.

A reference such as (Ref. Z3) means that some dimensions of the locomotive are given in Table 1 against Ref. Z3 but that the book contains no illustration of it.

NOTES ON DIMENSIONS QUOTED IN TABLE I *page 147*

The aim has been to give some idea of the size and possible power of each locomotive by means of a few dimensions.

In broad terms, grate area and adhesion weight are unavoidable limitations on sustained power output and sustained pull respectively, but any particular design of locomotive may have more restrictive limitations.

The driving–wheel diameter suggests whether the locomotive was intended for high speed or not. Equally important in this connection were the valve dimensions, but they were not usually published.

References from 1a to 16d are the plate numbers of the photographs; the Z numbers are associated with mentions in the text.

NOTE ON NOTATION

The group of locomotive wheels through which propulsive effort is applied to the rails are called 'coupled wheels' unless there was only one pair of them in which case they were called 'driving wheels'. Ahead of the coupled wheels might be others that carried weight and assisted in guiding the engine gently into curves. Behind the coupled wheels might be others that carried weight and perhaps conveyed some lateral restraint from the rails to the engine.

In the twentieth century came the Whyte system of defining the 'wheel arrangement' of locomotives by three (or four) numbers. The first and last are the numbers of wheels in the leading and trailing non-driving groups; the others are the number of coupled wheels in one (or two) intervening groups.

It is useful to add to the Whyte designation some information about the cylinders. In this book this is done by writing the number of cylinders and the sign / immediately before the numbers of wheels. Where no such preceding number appears, it is to be understood that the locomotive has two cylinders inside the frame and no others. The inclusion of C before / implies compound expansion in the cylinders.

The addition of T to the designation implies a tank engine with side-tanks, ST with a saddle-tank and WT with a well-tank.

I

STEAM ON RAILS

THE steam engine that could propel itself on rails and pull a load was essentially a nineteenth-century development but the first use of steam to produce controlled motion of solid bodies had been made some 1700 years earlier. Hero of Alexandria (AD 100) led steam through a hollow trunnion into a rotatable sphere whence it escaped through circumferentially pointing pipes and thus thrust them into rotation. This was the first steam turbine; it justifies mention here even though the steam turbine was never extensively employed as a propulsive agent on railways.

In the eighteenth century the 'atmospheric engine' was developed for working the large pumps required for lifting water out of mines. Its importance in the history of steam power is that it used steam and had a 'piston', a vital element in every steam engine of the conventional type.

A piston is a plug movable in a cylinder. In every position of the piston it must fit so closely that very little steam, water or air, ideally none, passes between the piston and the cylinder and yet must not fit so tightly that friction seriously opposes relative motion. Such precision of manufacture of a large cylinder and piston was impracticable before the nineteenth century and so the necessary condition was secured by cutting circumferential grooves in the piston and fitting each one with a hemp rope, or the like, sufficiently elastic to maintain contact with the cylinder wall, in spite of its geometrical imperfections, as the piston slid back and forth within it. This was a 'soft packing', an essential element in steam engines for a hundred years. It may seem a trivial detail to be mentioned at such an early stage in a review of a very wide subject, but it was in fact vital; the efficiency of every steam engine was limited by the efficiency of the means used for diminishing leakage of steam past pistons and valves. It was the development of high-precision machine tools in the nineteenth century and certain basic inventions (eg. that of the metallic 'piston ring' by Ramsbottom in 1850) that made the high-pressure high-speed steam engine practicable.

In the atmospheric engine, steam was allowed to enter a cylinder not primarily to push the piston but simply to sweep out the air. When that had been done, cold water was sprayed into the steam so that when in due course it was all condensed into water, the pressure in the cylinder was then about zero, and so the atmospheric pressure on the outside of the piston could force it inwards despite the resistance of the pump-bucket connected to it. Atmospheric engines (developed primarily by Newcomen) were necessarily slow and large in relation to the power they developed, but nothing better was known and by 1770 hundreds of them were at work in Great Britain. James Watt's invention of the separate condenser raised the efficiency of the atmospheric engine very considerably but it still had to be big because its propulsive pressure could not exceed that of the atmosphere, roughly 15 lb./in^2.

It was at about this time that it occurred to someone that as a shaft might be rotated by applying one's hand to a crank-handle, the backwards and forwards straight-line motion of an engine-piston could be used by means of a connecting-rod and crank to rotate a shaft. Next it was realised that if the boiler and everything else were made strong enough, steam pressure could be allowed to build up to any desired degree so that admission of steam to an engine-cylinder would not only sweep out the air but could exert on the piston a push strong enough for it to do useful work on its out-stroke in addition to what it did by virtue of atmospheric pressure on the in-stroke. If the steam pressure on the out-stroke were high enough, the atmospheric pressure became relatively unimportant and so a quite useful engine remained even if the condensing operation and the condenser were omitted. So after having pushed the piston along the cylinder, the steam could be allowed to escape into the atmosphere. In the 'double-acting' engine, steam was admitted to each end of the cylinder in turn and the piston was pushed by steam in each direction of motion in the cylinder. In this type of engine there must be a piston-rod extending from the piston through one of the end-walls of the cylinder in a 'gland' that permits relative motion without too much friction or too much leakage of steam, and so there must be a 'gland-packing'.

Double-acting atmospheric engines were made by Boulton & Watt in large numbers for industrial purposes but the company did not favour the use of any higher steam pressure than was needed by that type of engine. So it was still large and heavy in relation to its power as were the mine-pumping engines, and especially as the condenser was a large adjunct to the engine itself. But if a high boiler-pressure were used and the condenser cut out, the ratio of power to size could be drastically increased and indeed to the extent that if the engine and boiler were mounted on wheels it could be able to move itself and perhaps even pull a vehicle.

The names of Seguin (in France) and Murdock (in Cornwall) occur in this connection, but it was the Cornish mining engineer Richard Trevithick who, in conjunction with Andrew Vivian, built the first steam locomotive engine to carry passengers on a road; this was done at Camborne, Cornwall, in 1801. Later on Trevithick built the first steam engine to propel itself and a load of wagons on a metal track; this was done on the Penydarren tramway near Merthyr Tydvil, South Wales, in 1804. The track was made of flanged plates rather than rails as now commonly understood, but it is not unfair to accept Trevithick as the originator of 'steam on rails'. It must be added that the test-route, Penydarren to Abercynon, is so distinctly downhill that gravity alone would suffice for motion of modern vehicles on nicely laid rails, and so Trevithick's locomotive did not need to pull very hard to go down the primitive plateway. It did, however, take a train of empty wagons up a gradient of 1 in 18 at four mph.

It is interesting, although irrelevant, to add that in a few weeks Trevithick built the first steam railway locomotive to pull a pay-load solely to settle a bet between two Welsh industrialists; one was sure it could be done and the other was sure it couldn't. Some 500 guineas changed hands in consequence and the news induced some colliery men in other parts of Great Britain to try building steam engines for hauling coal in vehicles running on rails. The origins of steam on rails were thus closely related to coal-mining; this was convenient in that a steam engine's main needs are for coal and water, both readily available at colliery pit-heads.

In Trevithick's first engine, steam that had pushed the piston to either end of its stroke was then allowed to escape through a pipe that ended in the lower part of the chimney that conveyed hot gas upwards from the boiler to the open air. It was noticed that each puff of steam from the pipe hastened the draught on the fire and the flames brightened perceptibly. The same phenomenon was noticed by Hackworth in a locomotive he built some ten years later and even 30 years later still there continued profitless discussion as to who invented the 'blast-pipe' that was always the accepted means of providing the strong draught that every steam locomotive needed if it were to be commercially viable.

The very difficult task of making a consistent story out of recorded details of Trevithick's locomotive was undertaken by E. W. Twining and the result recorded in an article in the *Railway Magazine* for March 1951,

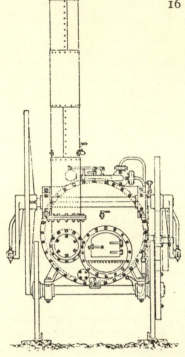

Fig. 2. The first steam on rails. Conjectural reconstruction of the form in which Richard Trevithick's engine ran as a locomotive on the Penydarren Tramroad in 1804, based on a careful consideration of contemporary evidence.

page 197 and illustrated by one of Mr Twining's beautiful drawings reproduced here as Fig. 2 on page 16-17. The Penydarren locomotive had a return-tube boiler with the chimney attached alongside the fire-hole. Having found it advantageous to enclose the cylinders of mine-pumping engines in steam-jackets, Trevithick placed the single cylinder of his locomotive engine inside the boiler and as the vehicle was to run nearly horizontally, he placed the cylinder horizontally, whereas normal mining engineering practice was to use vertical cylinders. The piston made a stroke of four feet, twice as long as that in eventual locomotive practice and the locomotive ran with a rather striking trombone action of its cross-head ahead of it. A connecting-rod on each side of the boiler worked cranks on the ends of a shaft extending across the locomotive between the chimney and the adjacent end of the boiler, and from that shaft the drive was taken to one of the four rail wheels by a train of three spur gears. The use of this gear-train may have discouraged the use of springs but at all events none were used and so the locomotive must have proceeded with a regular succession of severe jolts at the rail-joints each emphasised by a fierce spit of steam from the dead-weight loaded safety-valve.

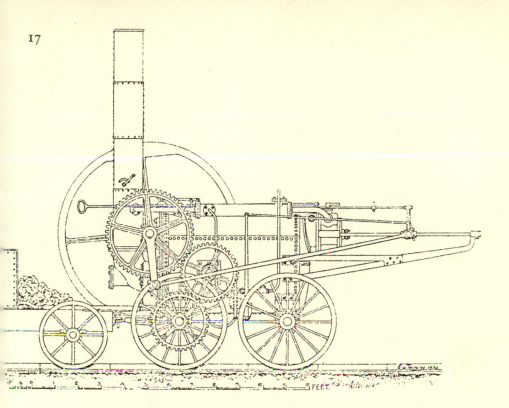

The probable reason for using a gear drive at all was that when the engine was at rest, axial movement of the intermediate gear disengaged it from the other two, and left the crankshaft free to be rotated by hands applied to the rim of the large wheel mounted on one end of it. This enabled the cranks to be set in a good position for starting and was a necessary provision as the locomotive would often stop with crank and connecting-rod so nearly in line that no practicable steam pressure could make it re-start.

The valve that fed steam to the ends of the cylinder remained stationary while the piston made the greater part of each stroke and was moved into position for the next stroke by a tappet as the crank approached each dead centre. There was no 'reversing gear'; direction of motion after each stop was selected by hand-setting the valve in the position for feeding steam to the appropriate end of the cylinder.

The exhaust steam was led by a pipe into the chimney and there went upwards and livened the draught on the fire to an extent noticed by Trevithick who did not, however, find any need to intensify the steam jet specifically as the boiler produced enough steam without it. In the chimney was a damper in the form of a plate that could be swung about a horizontal axis by use of a handle outside the chimney either to close the chimney or to leave it almost unobstructed. The damper was naturally below the exhaust-pipe and this is mentioned in notes made by Trevithick and repeated in Mr Twining's article, but by an oversight his drawing shows the damper above the pipe.

The Penydarren locomotive was a wonderful first placing of a steam engine on rails by an engineer with enough practical experience to be sure that it would run well enough and long enough to do a specific job. If Trevithick could have added to his genius the conviction and tenacity of purpose later to be shown by George Stephenson, steam might have been common on rails some 20 years earlier than was actually the case.

Contemporaneous with Trevithick was Murray, who built a two-cylinder engine with cranks at right angles in 1802, who invented the short D-valve known as the 'slide-valve' in 1806, and who with Blenkinsop at Leeds in 1812 placed steam on rails in a locomotive that had toothed wheels engaging with toothed track. It was soon established, however, that this admirably positive drive was superfluous on any gradient flatter than about 1 in 30. Smooth wheels on smooth rails (with sand when rails were greasy) sufficed for all ordinary railway traction.

From Trevithick in South Wales and Murray at Leeds, steam on rails spread to Northumberland where Hedley, Hackworth and George Stephenson, following Trevithick after an interval of about ten years, succeeded in building and running steam locomotives on colliery railways. Another ten years elapsed before the opening of the Stockton & Darlington Railway, mainly for minerals but available for all commercial purposes, and four years later came the famous 'Rainhill Trials' near Liverpool to convince everyone that steam on rails could revolutionise land transport. It had taken 25 years for a few persevering pioneers to accomplish a tremendous advance by modest detail departures from the design of Trevithick's locomotive of 1804.

The directors of the Liverpool & Manchester Railway, nearing completion in 1829, were not sure that motive power should be derived from locomotive engines but were prepared to be convinced by actual performance. They therefore offered a substantial prize of £500 for the builder of such an engine that should best perform a specified task that involved 10 trips in each direction over a length of about 1½ miles while moving 3.3 times its own weight at at least 10 mph. With astonishing generosity, for which locomotive engineers have always been grateful, they admitted locomotives as high as 15 feet. The winning locomotive, Stephenson's

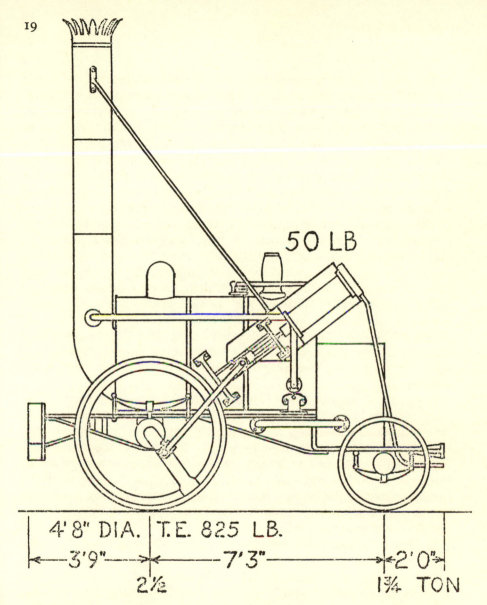

50 LB

4' 8" DIA. | T.E. 825 LB.

3'9" — 7'3" — 2'0"

2½

1¾ TON

Fig. 3. Stephenson's Rocket, *winner at Rainhill in 1829*

Rocket, took full advantage of this but it was found that performance of early steam locomotives was not impaired by restriction to a smaller height and 13½ ft became an accepted standard for British railways.

The *Rocket* had worthy competitors but none of them stayed the course without failure, whereas the *Rocket* went through unscathed at well above the specified speed. Its design was due to George Stephenson and his son Robert, but incorporated a vitally important feature in the multi-tubular boiler suggested by Henry Booth, the secretary of the company formed by the Stephensons, father and son, to build steam locomotives. A large factor in the success of the *Rocket* was its combination of multi-tubular boiler, water-wall fire-box and blast-pipe; in all subsequent history, few successful steam locomotives differed from it in any of these respects.

The *Rocket* differed from the Penydarren locomotive in having two cylinders and their pistons worked cranks set at right angles in two wheels that supported the leading axle. Each valve could be worked by either of two eccentrics, one for each direction of running, and the change from either to the other could be effected without much difficulty when the engine was stationary. Whatever the position of the cranks, the engine could start in one direction or the other and so there was no need for any parallel to Trevithick's scheme for disconnecting the connecting-rod from the track-wheels. The *Rocket* had no brakes and the method of stopping it after it had made a demonstration run at 30 mph is a matter for surmise.

A potentially serious competitor of the *Rocket* was Hackworth's *Sans Pareil*, a husky Northumbrian colliery engine with vertical cylinders which prohibited the use of springs for the directly-driven wheels, although they could have been applied to the other wheels. The rules of the competition insisted on springs and so it may be doubted whether any degree of excellence in haulage could have justified the award of the prize to Hackworth's engine. In the event, it was prevented from completing the course by mechanical defect, and in addition its fuel consumption was very much higher than that of the *Rocket*.

Breakdown of auxiliaries also defeated Braithwaite & Ericsson's *Novelty* which technically was very interesting in several ways. It was very much lighter than the other engines and it was in fact a road vehicle fitted with a steam engine rather than a big steam engine mounted on wheels. Trevithick had tried steam in a road vehicle in 1801. In 1824 Burstall and Hill designed a steam road-coach with the cardan-shaft drive that has characterised the vast majority of mechanically propelled road vehicles ever since, and by 1828 Gurney was running road coaches with steam cylinders and pistons directly driving the cranked rear axle. These road vehicles were of much lighter construction than the colliery engines and

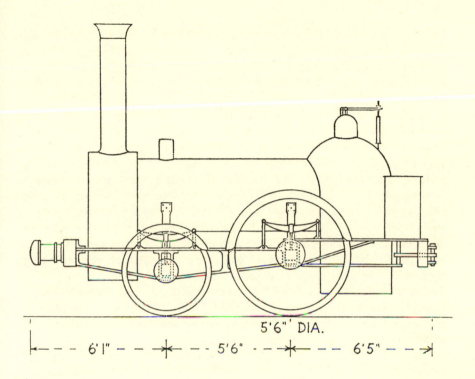

5'6" DIA.

6' I" — 5'6" — 6'5"

Fig. 4. Bar-frame 2–2–0 (Edward Bury)

Robert Stephenson had realised that in that respect they were superior. This reflection influenced the design of the *Rocket*, which was lighter than its Stephenson predecessors, but had nevertheless sufficient guts (George Stephenson's word) to survive the 30-mile test specified at Rainhill without breaking down.

The *Rocket's* performance convinced a majority of the Liverpool & Manchester Railway directors that they could safely go ahead with reliance on locomotive engines, but a minority would have preferred stationary engines to rotate drums that could pull trains intermittently by means of wire-ropes. Deprived of this alternative, the minority took solace in opposing purchase of locomotives from the Stephensons. In this way Edward Bury came into prominence as a builder of locomotives that differed importantly, and in some ways regrettably, in details of construction from the *Rocket* and its immediate successors from the Stephenson works.

Bury mounted the boiler on a 'bar frame' and placed the cylinders inside the frame with connecting-rods driving a cranked axle, whereas the *Rocket's* cylinders were 'outside' the wheels and its connecting-rods drove crankpins projecting from the bosses of the wheels. The Bury layout markedly reduced the action of the mechanism in swaying (sideways oscillation in opposite directions front and back) any short four-wheel locomotive. The value of this when running fast was so great in conjunction with a possible gain from warmer location of the cylinders in the smoke-box that the Stephensons had adopted inside cylinders (first in *Planet* built in 1830) in spite of the difficulty and expense of making a reliable cranked axle to go with them. In consequence inside cylinders became an accepted feature in British locomotive design for 70 years and more. In a hundred years it could be discerned that outside cylinders might have been better after all; in North America, for example, very little use was made of inside cylinders after the 1840s, except in New England.

The first locomotives had only four wheels (they could not have had fewer) and Edward Bury guided himself almost to a dead-end by limiting himself to that number. In the eight-wheel locomotive that came in later years, the greater length reduced the swaying effect of outside cylinders so much that they became practicable even for fast running. They were adopted in America and with bar frames (derived from those used by Bury) they characterised American practice to the end of steam on rails.

The Stephensons at first used double plate frames and four 'axle-boxes' (bearings) for a cranked axle so that even if it broke in the middle it might still keep its wheels on the rails. This started the vogue of double frames extensively adopted in Great Britain. The Stephensons on the other hand had found in a few years that cranked axles could be made sufficiently reliable to be used with single plate frames. They then abandoned double frames and British railways gradually followed them in this respect, although the Great Western Railway built such frames as late as 1909 and were using some over 30 years later still.

A four-wheel locomotive, while admirably simple, could never be a happy fast runner unless restricted to a very small size. The cylinders had to be ahead of the leading axle and the fire-box had to be behind the other axle.

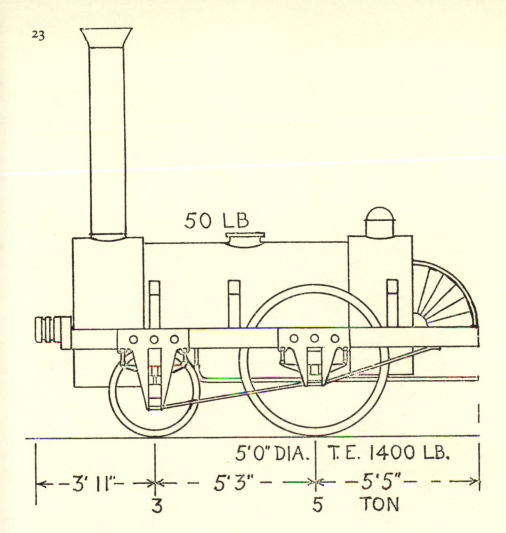

50 LB

5'0" DIA. | T.E. 1400 LB.

←—3' 11"—→|←— 5'3" —→|←— 5'5" —→|
3   5   TON

Fig. 5. Stephenson's Planet, 1830

So a fair proportion of the total weight was outside its wheel base. The bigger the engine, the more pronounced this effect, and so a four-wheeler would 'porpoise' over ups and downs in the track, and would sway even on good straight track.

In a six-wheeler on the other hand the fire-box was naturally set between the second and third axles and so 'overhang' was limited to the front end; with inside cylinders such overhang need not be great. So six-wheelers became common in the 1830s and 60 years elapsed before eight-wheel tender-engines began to become numerous in Britain. In the nineteenth century, the typical British locomotive was a six-wheeler with or without a tender. Hundreds of the latter variety, known as 'tank engines' because the water-tank (and a coal-bunker) was on the engine itself and not on a separate vehicle, were being built even as late as the 1950s.

For a time the Stephensons built 'long-boiler' six-wheel engines, with the fire-box behind the rear axle. This design, necessarily limited to small fire-boxes and low speeds, had a vogue for mineral traffic but it was less satisfactory than the conventional six-wheeler.

In early American railroad development, Col. John Stevens and his son Robert L Stevens had eminence comparable with that of George Stephenson and his son Robert in Britain, and an historic event was the purchase in 1831 of a 2–2–0 *John Bull* by the Stevens from the Stephensons for use on the Camden & Amboy Rail Road. An innovation applied to *John Bull* after trial in service was an additional two-wheel leading truck primarily to act as a cow catcher but also arranged to guide the locomotive into curves. This modification was necessary for running on the rather lightly laid tracks common in early American railroad practice but it was retained even when tracks were made good and so leading trucks were normal in the New World.

Although the earliest locomotives to be used in America had come from Britain, American engineers soon got into their own stride and methods in designing and building locomotives and also in exporting them. By 1840 William Norris of Philadelphia had supplied seventeen 2/4–2–0 locomotives to the Birmingham & Gloucester Railway and these engines are still famed in British railway history for their success in climbing two miles at 1 in 38 on the 'Lickey Bank' between Bromsgrove and Birmingham.

By 1840 there had been many American experiments in wheel arrangements, cylinder arrangements, boilers, frames and so on, but the 2/4–4–0 was already becoming recognised as the most generally useful form of locomotive for American conditions.

British locomotives were criticised as being unnecessarily difficult to repair and it became the prime aim in American design to avoid any such charge. Because of this, it soon became standard American practice to use outside cylinders with overhead valves, worked through rocking shafts, by valve gear inside the frame. A four-wheel leading bogie gave single-point support at the front end and equalising levers (used by Hackworth as far back as 1827) provided two-point support by the four coupled wheels. Three-point support is the ideal for firm mounting and its advantage was greater on American tracks than on the better-laid ones in Britain. Wooden frames, wrought–iron plate frames and wrought–iron bar frames were all well tried and the last-named persisted as the American standard with iron replaced by steel when that material became the less expensive. Broadly speaking the Stephenson type of boiler used in *Planet* was accepted, generally with raised outer fire-box.

The foregoing review is limited to remarks on the general layout of the locomotive and says little about constructional details which did, however, present quite formidable difficulties to the pioneer builders. Of readily available materials, which was the best to use for making the boiler barrel ? – the fire-box ? – the tubes ? – the cylinders ? – and so on. Then with the material of the barrel decided, how thick should the plate be to stand such-and-such pressure and to last for so many years ? If a change in type of fuel were to be made, would it demand a change in material for the inner fire-box ? Where mechanical components slid in loaded contact, what combination of materials would suffer least wear ? What should be used as lubricant ? Many questions of this kind had to be asked and the answers found by slow, costly and even dangerous trial.

Some of these questions were never answered in any absolutely certain way, but as the years went by, experience provided fairly reliable guidance although still leaving room for differences of opinion. In the 1830s however, intelligence, mechanical instinct, observation and perseverance had to be applied to the utmost in developing the steam locomotive into a reliable machine for profitable sale and use.

Development of the steam locomotive in size meant more than four wheels and throughout the history of steam on British rails after about 1840, the large majority of the locomotives were six-wheelers. Their wheel arrangements were 2–2–2, 2–4–0, 0–4–2 or 0–6–0; of these there were more 0–6–0s and fewer 0–4–2s than any others. At all times the 0–6–0s well outnumbered every other wheel arrangement. Even after nationalisation of British railways in 1948, large numbers of 0–6–0 tank engines were built to what was essentially a nineteenth–century design of the Great Western Railway. If in examination of locomotive development, attention were confined to the most numerously represented form, the tale could be short and dull as the conventional 0–6–0 changed only very little in a century. For example over two thousand 0–6–0s built between 1857 and 1942 to designs produced by the Midland Railway were identical in axle-spacing (8 ft and 8 ft 6 in.). Over that range of engines the grate area (a basic limitation on boiler power) rose only from $15\frac{1}{2}$ to 21 sq. ft.

The London & North Western Railway built nearly two thousand 0–6–0 engines, 943 of one class. The Paris, Lyons & Mediterranean Railway had over a thousand identical 0–6–0s.

In North America the 0–6–0 was purely a 'switching' (shunting) engine. Every American 'road engine' had to have a leading truck or bogie and the 2–6–0 with outside cylinders was the counterpart of the conventional British 0–6–0 with inside cylinders.

The Stephensons' *Rocket* that showed everyone at Rainhill what a steam locomotive could do, ran on rails separated by 4ft 8½in. and the gaily serrated top of its chimney was nearly 15 ft above the rails. The rail-gauge became a world-standard (in the sense that it was used for most of the mileage) and in Britain the permissible maximum height on most railways was between 13 ft and 13 ft 6 in, while the allowable maximum width was about 8 ft 10 in. Till the end of steam, locomotives intended to run in Great Britain were limited to these dimensions and also had less easily definable weight restrictions. On each railway there was a specific top limit to the load permitted on any axle and also a restriction determined by the loadings and positions of adjacent axles. With the gradual introduction of stronger rails, the allowable axle-loadings rose as time went on, but designers always found need to go right up to the permissible limit and to press for relaxation of it.

More powerful locomotives were necessarily heavier and before the end of the nineteenth century the biggest British locomotives had to have at least eight wheels each. On the passenger side, 4–4–0s were becoming common and 4–4–2s and 4–6–0s were soon to follow. For goods trains heavier than 0–6–0s could expeditiously handle, 0–8–0s were running before 1900 and 2–8–0s came in the next few years. Every engine had to have at least two cylinders and few were given any more.

From then till World War I ten-wheelers were developed by most of the larger British railways, compound expansion in three or four cylinders was tried, and there was a more enduring move to simple expansion in three or four cylinders in some of the largest locomotives for passenger-trains.

In the full life of steam on British railways, the largest locomotives for passenger trains were six-coupled and for freight trains eight-coupled. Exceptions were the 3/2–8–2s used by the LNER on passenger trains between Edinburgh and Aberdeen in 1934-44 and, occasionally on British Railways, the 2/2–10–0s developed by R. A. Riddles. Permissible axle-loading had risen to 22½ tons and locomotive weights to about 108 tons; the corresponding world maxima (in the United States of America) were

37 and 276 tons. Articulated locomotives were in a different category; for them the maxima were 178 tons (the LNE 6/2–8–8–2, Ref. 14d) in Britain and 345 (the 24 Union Pacific 4/4–8–8–4s, Ref. Z15) in the United States.

It is interesting to reflect that each significant change in rail-traction occupied a lifetime. Superheating, known and tried on stationary engines before the *Rocket* was built, did not start to 'take on' in locomotive practice for 65 or 70 years. At about the same time the compression-ignition engine (conveniently but not quite accurately called the 'diesel') had become practicable and in another 65 years it was clearly about to displace steam as the main tractive power on railways.

During the first of these 65-year periods, boiler pressures in steam locomotives rose from 40 to about 200 lb per sq in.; in the second the rise was to about 250, although here and there 300 was used out of necessity and not because it had any peculiar advantage.

By 1850 certain Great Western trains had averaged a mile a minute between Paddington and Didcot (53 miles) but it was not until nearly 1900 that any passenger train in the world was advertised to run at that rate from start to stop. By 1939 Britain had a few daily trains booked at speeds of about 70 mph but most passenger trains averaged less than 60 mph. The same general level applied in France, Germany and the USA with perhaps some superiority in the fastest trains. American passenger trains and locomotives were about twice as heavy as in Britain.

Broad trends in the development of steam on rails were few, slight and slow after about 1845; the pattern had been set by then and although for ever afterwards experimental departures from it were being tried, at the end the steam locomotive was an elongated *Rocket* with a superheater and piston valves. It was bigger and was commonly worked much harder, but it had to have a few hours rest every day while men did some dirty work in removing waste products from smoke-box and ashpan, and a day's rest every week while sludge and scale were got out of the boiler.

Its valves and pistons needed examination at intervals of about 25,000 miles and it needed complete dismantling and thorough overhaul every 75,000 miles or so. From about 1940, great efforts were made to increase the mileage that could be run between major repairs by special attention to details in design, material and maintenance. Some classes of engine exceeded 100,000 miles but the majority did not. These figures are interesting in suggesting comparisons between locomotives of different classes but they tell nothing about the cost of repairs. If for example repairs after 100,000 miles were twice as costly as those after 50,000 miles, the advantage of the former would be limited to that of reduced unavailability of the engine.

During the last half-century of steam the appearance of locomotives of successive designs on any one railway did not alter much except in respect of size because the important changes were either unnoticeable or invisible. So while this book contains pictures of typical examples of the steam locomotive and some figures for its growth, it has to examine the subject in some detail in order to find more than one or two developments during a century.

Development right at the end was in detail design and choice of materials to minimise wear and corrosion and to simplify removal of ash, char and dirt of other descriptions. One design might be superior in power, speed and economy to another for reasons quite unrelated to any differences in their published dimensions. Anyone who failed to realise this, might well ascribe the absence of any discernible relation between published performance and published dimensions to some supernatural characteristic in the steam locomotive and be accordingly fascinated by it. But even those who were professionally engaged in design, building and running of steam locomotives could develop quite irrational ideas. One might hear it stoutly stated, for example, that while a driving-wheel diameter of 81 in. could be all right in the south of England, nothing bigger than 78 in. was any good in Scotland.

Even textbooks and test-reports could reveal imperfect comprehension of basic essentials and so it may reasonably be concluded that the steam locomotive (like many another piece of mechanism) could be designed and built on the basis of experience to work satisfactorily without demanding any real understanding of its physical fundamentals. Its adherent adaptability and that of the men who worked it could offset considerable imperfection in design and construction.

2
BOILER AND FITTINGS

FOR feeding the earliest stationary steam engines, the boiler was a roughly cylindrical vessel straddling brick-walls between which was the fire. Size and weight did not matter very much, but simplicity of the metal parts was important and the cylindrical form was the best in this respect.

Later on, it became the practice to build the fire on a grate inside a tube within the cylindrical shell of the boiler and therefore surrounded by water. This was excellent in making sure that what heat passed through the wall of the inner tube was bound to be caught by the water. But the gases that left the fire-bed were still very hot when they came to the end of the inner tube and, to secure some of their heat, an early artifice was to guide the gases into a parallel tube in which they returned, within the boiler shell, to the fireman's end of the boiler. At that point they passed into a vertical chimney which created the draught required to keep the fire going.

This 'return-tube' type of boiler was not easy to make even by the best techniques known in the eighteenth century. Cast iron was used because of the comparative ease with which it can be made into any shape that can be formed in a wooden pattern, but it is a brittle material, liable to failure without warning if overstressed, and a few boiler explosions sufficed to convince most engineers that it was less expensive in the long run to make boilers rather toilsomely from bent and rivetted wrought-iron plates.

Trevithick's locomotive (p. 16) had a rivetted boiler of the return-tube type. The chimney and fire-door were thus at the same end of the boiler, with supplies of fuel and water on a closely adjacent four-wheel tender. On an intermediate platform there was room for a man or men to stand and to carry out the separate duties of driver and fireman; the primary care of the latter was always to be sure that the boiler contained enough water to cover the internal tube as otherwise the fire inside it could overheat the upper part of the tube into a condition of dangerous weakness. It would be inconvenient if he forgot the fire; it could be fatal if he forgot the water.

The pressure of steam in the boiler could attain (for example) 40 lb. per sq. in. and this was sufficient to spread a great deal of death and destruction in the neighbourhood if any part of the boiler should 'let go'. The young man who, over a century later, once dismissed such a pressure as harmless because it was 'less than three times atmospheric' had not quite grasped the essential mechanics of the situation that could have arisen if he had not been prevented from unscrewing a washout plug in a boiler.

The return-tube type of boiler used in most of the early steam locomotives was not very efficient because the total area of the surface licked by the hot gases on their way from the fire-bed to the chimney was not great enough to extract much of their heat from them. There was a need to increase this 'heating surface' without having to use a very long boiler. Inspiration for a solution to this problem came just in time to enable it to be applied by the Stephensons in the boiler of the *Rocket*, built to be a competitor in the Rainhill trials of 1829. Instead of passing the hot gases through a single wide flue, the Stephensons drew them through a number of parallel tubes, no longer than the flue but having a much greater total area of wall. This constituted a 'multitubular boiler'; the tubes were called 'fire-tubes' because the hot gases passed inside them.

Later came 'water-tube' boilers (never much used on locomotives) in which the tubes contained the water that was to be boiled by heat from gases licking the outside surfaces of the tubes. Although repeatedly tried for more than a century on locomotives, water-tube boilers failed to justify themselves in that service. One difficulty was that of removing from the inside of the tubes the scale deposited by impurities in the water. Where, as in stationary steam-plant and on board ship, the steam is condensed and the same water repeatedly re-used, scale formation can be reduced to a negligible rate, but that is impossible on a non-condensing steam locomotive. Another disadvantage of the water-tube boiler as applied in locomotives was that it required a very great weight of fire-brick to make fire-box walls thick enough to prohibit excessive loss of heat.

With the Stephensons' boiler-barrel occupied by a bundle of fire-tubes, it was convenient to have the fire in a separate box made with double walls enclosing water to be boiled by heat from the fire. A pipe led water from the boiler barrel to the bottom of the fire-box water-space and another pipe led steam from the top of the fire-box to the top part of the boiler.

THE CONVENTIONAL LOCOMOTIVE BOILER

The design of the *Rocket's* boiler represented perhaps the biggest single technological advance in the history of the steam locomotive. With one modification (incorporated in the Stephensons' immediate successor to the *Rocket*) it formed the model for all subsequent locomotive boilers. The modification was to give the boiler barrel a backward prolongation that was also extended downwards to form an 'outer fire-box' and to insert in the extension a slightly smaller 'inner fire-box' which contained the fire. The fire-tubes extended from the front plate of the inner fire-box to the front end plate of the boiler-barrel and the still warm (or hot) gases were caught in the smoke-box and flowed thence through the chimney into the open air.

Fig. 6. Boiler of GN Atlantic (Ref. 4b)

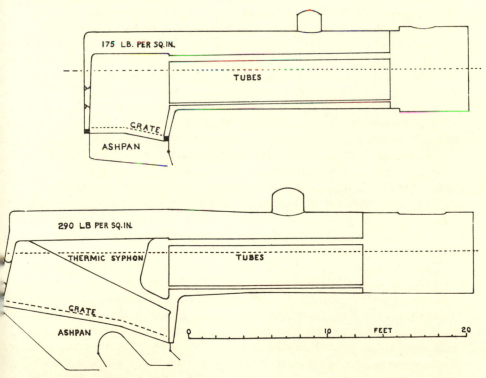

Fig. 7. Boiler of Chapelon 4–8–0 (Ref. 16b)

The cylindrical forms of the barrel and the tubes were strong in resisting the pressure of steam and water on them. The flat plates of the fire-box, however, did not have that advantage and were therefore given mutual support by interconnecting rods called 'stays'. Stays turned out to be far more troublesome in service than might reasonably have been expected and remained so throughout the history of the steam locomotive. They were retained only because no superior alternative was ever devised. Difficulties with stays and other vulnerable parts of the conventional locomotive boiler were intensified with rise in working pressure. From the 50 lb. per sq. in. of the *Rocket* in 1829, working pressures gradually rose to about 200 lb. per sq. in. in 1900. In Great Britain there was some use of 250 lb. per sq. in. after 1926; experiments with 280 lb. per sq. in. were abandoned.

In the bottom of the fire-box was an assembly of iron bars set parallel with intervening spaces to form a fire-grate. Well below the fire-grate was the ashpan provided to retain the ash and cinders that dropped between the grate-bars and also to exclude air from the underside of the fire when the damper-doors were closed. The ashpan was a bit of ironmongery that seemed to demand little attention in design or construction. Designers treated it with less respect than they might have done if it had been a practice to include in each ashpan-drawing a picture of the heap of ash that could build in it during a long run with dirty coal. Some of the large locomotives built a century after the *Rocket* could be strangled by ash in their inadequate ashpans. The very last locomotives to be built by British Railways (the Class 9 2/2-10-0s, 1954 to 1960) suffered in this way. Designers tended to hope that ash would slide down rough steel inclined at 30 degrees to the horizontal, whereas it can in fact cling quite tenaciously even to nearly vertical surfaces. For most of the history of steam on British rails the coal did not make much ash, and its disposal created no serious problem when labour was plentiful. But conditions changed and the end of steam was hastened by the volume of dirty waste products of the inferior coal that became common.

The ash in some types of coal could melt in the heart of the fire and drop down to the fire-bars, where in the cold, incoming air it would solidify and form a gradually widening cake of clinker that would eventually block the grate entirely. For more than a century, coals of this objectionable type could be kept away from British locomotives, but elsewhere it was otherwise and as a means of alleviating the difficulty, a fire-grate might be in the form of bars about eight inches long, each rockable about a transverse horizontal axis. The bars in such a 'rocking-grate' could be rocked

a. GC single-wheeler No. 969 as running in 1915

b. Later form of LNW saddle-tank designed in 1863

c. GW steam rail-motor coach (1903-34)

d. GN steam rail-motor coach (1905-26)

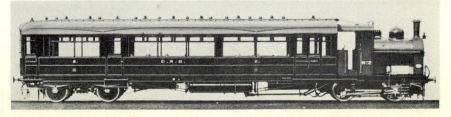

Plate 1

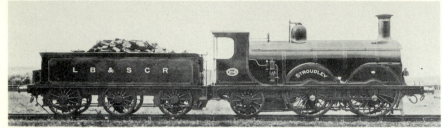

a. *Hardwicke*, star performer in the 1895 Race to Scotland

b. LBS No. 184. The 78-in. wheels were the largest in a British 0–4–2

c. GW double-frame 4–4–0 *City of Truro*. Touched about 100 mph downhill in 1904

d. NB No. 491, a typical Scottish 4–4–0

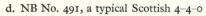

Plate 2

in groups by hand operation of a lever in the cab, and this could break up
clinker before it got too thick. Rocking-grates were not uncommon overseas in the nineteenth century, but never numerous in Britain before the
1950s, when the National Coal Board was producing inferior coal and
promising worse.

In the early days, outer fire-boxes might be extended upwards (in 'hay-
stack' form) to provide plenty of space for steam, but the advantage, never
very great, obtainable from this diminished as boiler barrels were made in
such large diameters as to leave little room for upward extension of the
fire-box.

In its lower part, a fire-box might be wide and shallow or narrow and
deep, as permitted by the adjoining wheels, but over the whole life of
the steam locomotive after 1830, the longitudinal section of the boiler
never differed substantially in general form from that shown in Fig. 1, p.8.

An importation from Belgium was the Belpaire form of outer fire-box
of which the upper part has vertical flat sides and a flat top parallel to the
crown sheet of the inner fire-box which can thus be tied to the outer fire-
box by stays that are at right angles to the plates that they connect. In
Britain, the Belpaire fire-box was adopted as standard by the Great Central
Railway, the Great Western Railway and later by the Midland Railway;
in America, the Pennsylvania Rail Road used it extensively. In a big boiler
that was set near the top limit of the loading gauge, the side sheets of
a Belpaire fire-box could not be quite parallel, and this diminished its
advantage.

From America came the 'wide fire-box' entirely above the frame-plates
and therefore not limited, as was the conventional 'narrow fire-box', to an
outside width of about four feet. In the wide fire-box, the grate could be
twice as wide as in the narrow box and this enabled a large grate-area to
be provided without undue length. In Britain a wide fire-box had to be
behind the coupled wheels of an express train engine whose rear end had
therefore to be supported by non-driving wheels. In America the extra
three feet in permissible height enabled wide fireboxes to be placed over
wheels as large as seven feet.

Because the gases in the fire-tubes had cooled considerably before they
reached the smoke-box, the water was boiling far less violently at that end
of the boiler than it was at the fire-box. So while it was thought desirable to
have a clear height of about two feet above the fire-box so that steam in
that vicinity should not be completely mixed with splashes and bursting
bubbles, a smaller clear height would suffice at the smokebox end of the

barrel, which might therefore be made in tapered form. The advantage of this was a small saving in weight and a slightly broadened view for the driver. The tapered boiler was first extensively used in North America and appeared as a novelty in Britain when Churchward on the Great Western introduced his new designs, based in several ways on American practice, in 1903. It became a standard feature of Great Western engines and, 30 years later, was virtually adopted by the LMS.

SAFETY VALVES

In the early days of the stationary steam boiler, the safety-valve was a conical plug fitting on to the conical end of a passage leading from the boiler and pressed down into firm contact by a weight, unless the steam pressure under the valve was high enough to sustain the weight, in which case it lifted the valve out of contact with the seating and steam 'blew' through a very narrow gap into the open air. On a locomotive this device was defective in that every jolt from the track tended to unseat the valve and thus to cause a momentary loss of steam. The remedy was to replace the weight by a spring and this was done by Fenton in 1812. Subsequent safety-valves showed only unnecessary and insignificant departures from what Fenton had done. In the Salter safety-valve (Fig. 8) the spring could be light because it worked with a lever. In the Ramsbottom safety-valve (Fig. 9) one strong spring held down two separate valves; the bridging piece had a long tail, extended in some cases into the cab. The object of this was to enable the driver to reduce the load on each valve in turn by up-and-down blows on the tail. This he might do if he had any suspicion that the valves had become 'stuck' and were not lifting when they should. (On the LNW, enginemen would have found it hard to reach the safety-valve tail, as it did not extend into the cab.)

On the other hand, it was a common drivers' offence to overload safety-valves so that they might have at their command a higher boiler-pressure than the designer had intended. This was frowned upon as being inherently dangerous and some ingenuity was expended on designing safety-valves so that they could not be unofficially overloaded. On the LNW, Francis Webb encased Ramsbottom safety-valves in a way that was regarded as successful in this respect on the dubious ground that no-one ever claimed the prize that was offered to the inventor of any proved overloading dodge.

In the nineteenth century it was not uncommon for a locomotive to have just one driver for a period of years, (on some railways a locomotive normally limited to one driver would have his name painted inside its cab). If he was

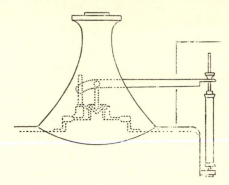

Fig. 8. Salter safety-valve in tall casing

a believer in overloading safety-valves, he would take care that for some time after the engine was placed in service new, or newly repaired, the boiler pressure was never allowed to rise to the 'blowing-off' point. This could allow the valves to become 'stuck' by corrosion associated with the inevitable very slight leakage of steam, and the engineman would *not* use the tail, or anything else, to unstick them. After a few months this passive offence might enable the safety-valves to 'hold' against a good deal more than the official working pressure.

In Great Britain, a notable feature of the later history of the safety-valve was a fashion that persisted after a sudden start in 1920 for using the old 'pop' safety-valve. Ascribed to G. W. Richardson of the Troy & Boston Rail Road, and dated 1866, this was an invention that was *not* mothered by necessity. It arose from ingenuity applied to a problem that it was never necessary to solve for any practical reason.

When the regulator was closed on a locomotive with full boiler pressure and a very hot fire, the safety-valve would 'blow' and discharge steam much faster than usual. This meant that the boiler pressure was higher than that at which the safety-valve blew lightly. Someone imagined that this difference was a danger, whereas it was never more than trifling compared

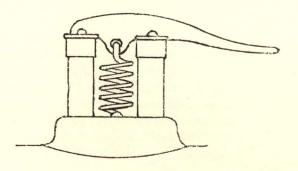

Fig. 9. Typical Ramsbottom safety-valve

with the margin of strength of the boiler over the official working pressure. (It is common in every technology to find someone making a fuss about something but carefully avoiding any reference to its negligible magnitude.)

But a safety-valve was specially designed and made so that the first dribble of steam past it was caused to push an additional surface and thus to open the valve wider. When the pressure had dropped by about 2 lb. per sq. in. the valve would close suddenly and completely. Instead of the continuous hiss of the ordinary safety-valve when blowing, the pop-valve produced a succession of what were in the early days 'pops' but in high-pressure maturity, explosions. To achieve this was quite a feat in design and construction; it fired the imagination of other inventors and there was a lot of American litigation over patents on products of ingenuity misplaced on this subject.

There was never any need for the pop safety-valve and indeed the Great Western Railway, even after a trial of one of them early in the twentieth century, never used it. Ordinary safety-valve noise is a nuisance, but the 'on and off' noise of the pop-valve was always worse. The use of the word 'silenced' in connection with the Ross pop-valve introduced in Britain in 1915-20 drew attention to this. But there was no pretence about silence once the pop-valve had become accepted in Britain. Its sudden outbursts at 180 lb. per sq. in. were bad enough to endure; at 250 lb. per sq. in. they were shattering and ought to have been outlawed. No matter how deep one's affection for the Age of Steam, one must condemn the pop safety-valve as an outrage against users of railway stations. Technically it was an atrocious waster of steam as it would often continue to blow until the boiler pressure was down by 20 lb. per sq. in., let alone two.

Disastrous failure of safety-valves to keep boiler pressure down were very rare after the very early days of steam, but one occurred on the LNW as late as November 1921.

CONSTRUCTION OF BOILER

Early boilers were made of wrought-iron plates bent to the right form and rivetted together; a specially awkward part was the junction of the underside of the barrel and the front plate of the outer fire-box. In the late nineteenth century means were developed for making mild steel less expensively than wrought iron; so the former superseded the latter and became available in large plate-form so convenient for making boilers that it was known as 'boiler-plate'.

To conserve heat, the boiler barrel and the upper part of the outer fire-box were, in later practice, covered by 'mattresses' of asbestos-like material about three inches thick, and this 'lagging' was enclosed in thin steel 'lagging-plates' bent to cylindrical form. They were held in position by a steel 'lagging-band' about three inches wide covering each line of contact between adjacent lagging-plates. Some builders used cheap lagging material of which they were not proud, but air was the cheapest of all and it was adopted in 'Austerity' 2/2–8–0s built in Britain during World War II.

Any finger that touched a lagging-plate of a boiler in steam might be dirtied but not burnt. Radiation from the smoke-box (not usually lagged) was usually sufficient to dissuade anyone from touching it by hand. Lagging-plates were commonly painted in glossy colour but smoke-boxes were too hot for anything but dull black. If a smoke-box door leaked near the bottom, the inflowing air would often arouse the char inside to a bright red heat that no paint could withstand and the affected area of steel retained a rust-like coating of red oxide of iron until the fault had been corrected and the burnt area re-painted. A red-hot smoke-box door was a sign that it was leaking air and not, as was often assumed, that the engine was working specially hard.

The inner fire-box was a strange component in that British practice was to make it of copper whereas steel was the common material for it almost everywhere else in the world. Copper was always very much more expensive than steel, but a copper fire-box lasted much longer than the corresponding steel one and it happened that the ultimate overall costs (so far as they could be ascertained) were so nearly equal that tradition was as important as anything else in deciding which to use. Stays were commonly made of cuprous material until it was found that in some parts of the fire-box the less expensive steel could be made to survive quite well. Similarly, fire-tubes were usually made of brass in the early days, but steel eventually became universal for this purpose.

DOME

In a hard-working boiler the water seethes very violently, and it was natural to seek dry steam by building on the boiler barrel an upward extension with domed top to provide a high place where steam could be collected well away from the water. So domes were common, but not universal. Some engineers found (or decided) that a well perforated pipe fixed inside the boiler barrel right at the top could collect steam well enough for the purpose and therefore that no dome was necessary. Eventually it became common practice to use a dome but the Great Western Railway was distinctive in that it had a middle period in which it used large and small domes in endless variety and profusion, between initial and final periods during which domeless boilers were standard.

In the late history of the steam locomotive many boilers were so large that there was no room for any high dome on top and when the water level had been allowed to rise above its normal upper limit there arose a serious risk that a lot of water would be carried with the steam into the cylinders, there, by its virtual incompressibility, to damage cylinder-covers, pistons or piston-rods. This happened to a BR 'Britannia' in its early days and led to changes in the design of the steam-collector.

The 'regulator' (the valve that controlled the flow of steam from the boiler to the cylinders) was placed in the dome if the boiler had one, but in the smoke-box if it hadn't. It would be hard to say which of those two positions offered the greatest difficulty of access to the regulator. On the smaller locomotives the regulator was usually easily and sensitively movable by the driver. Some types of regulator on the larger British locomotives were so hard to work that it was often necessary for both driver and fireman to strain simultaneously at two handles to make the desired change in regulator-opening. At the other extreme, the regulator standardised on the Great Western Railway in the twentieth century was so well designed, made and lubricated that a finger-and-thumb hold on its handle was strong enough to move it to any desired position. No virtue was discerned in this by the general run of locomotive designers, some of whom had never ridden on a locomotive.

FEED OF WATER TO BOILER

Until 1859 every locomotive boiler was fed with water by a pump (or pumps) worked by some part of the mechanism (usually a crosshead) and therefore operable only when the engine was travelling. Occasionally there arose a need to get more water into the boiler of a locomotive so hemmed in with vehicles that it could not travel; a useful dodge was to oil the treads of the driving wheels so that steam in the cylinders could rotate them (and work the pump) while the engine remained at rest under restraint by the brakes on the tender. The ball valve, invented by Melling, was first applied to locomotive feed water pumps on the Liverpool & Manchester Railway.

In British military history, the year 1759 was a 'year of miracles'. In French technological history the year 1859 marked the miracle of invention by Giffard of the combination of co-axial cones called the 'injector'. It enables the steam to leave a boiler, to suck up a lot of cold water and to take it, nicely warmed, back into the same boiler. The injector, once 'set', has no moving parts and it uses no power. All it receives it pushes into the boiler, where it is wanted; nothing is wasted. As an offset to this perfection, early injectors were sensitive to otherwise imperceptible variations in external conditions, but with persevering study of operation of injectors this effect was overcome. In particular, an early design used by Webb on the London & North Western Railway was accepted with such confidence that it was sealed and mounted so that it could be reached only with great difficulty and could be dismantled only after removal from the engine and transfer to Crewe Works. It was never surpassed in ease of operation and complete reliability.

By contrast, the 'exhaust steam injector' (developed near the end of the nineteenth century) which could save about seven per cent. of fuel by using some of the exhaust steam to heat the feed water, remained temperamental throughout its history and so was specifically excluded from the British Railways standard locomotive designs developed in 1950-60.

Other feed-water heating systems applied to locomotives used steam-driven pumps rather than injectors, which could be really reliable only with cold feed-water. Such systems might save ten per cent. of fuel, but this was so severely offset by their maintenance cost that many of them were abandoned. None persisted in Great Britain.

Injectors could be put out of action by solid matter that might be brought into them by the feed-water. Each locomotive had two injectors and simultaneous failure of both was rare, but when it did happen, the water in the boiler had to be conserved by stopping all flow of steam from it so that unless the train were running downhill it had soon to stop. Then if the fire were so hot that loss of steam through the safety-valves was causing the boiler water-level to fall, the fire had to be 'dropped' by using the drop-grate if the engine had one, or by pushing it through a hole made by lifting a few fire-bars out if the pricker could be got through the space between two of them, or by the plutonic herculean operation of lifting it out in laborious shovelfuls. Use of the drop-grate was easy enough if it was in proper working order, but on one occasion when it was incautiously done over track-sleepers soaked with oil from standing locomotives, the conflagration drove everyone away and burned all the paint off the locomotive.

WATER-LEVEL IN BOILER

So unreliability of injectors was a worry for enginemen and that it could occur in the middle of the twentieth century, 80 years after the origin of the unfailing LNW injector, was an indictment of something somewhere. A closely associated matter was reliability of the means of showing the level of the water in the boiler by means of gauge glasses. There was not much to criticise in this respect provided that firemen blew steam and water through the glasses at short intervals of time, by use of cocks provided for the purpose, in order to prohibit false readings by build-up of sludge in the connecting passages.

A safeguard against firemen's forgetfulness about water-level was the 'fusible plug' (Gurney 1826), a piece of metal of low melting point fitted into the most vulnerable plate of the inner firebox. Overheating of the plate caused the plug to melt at a temperature not high enough to weaken the plate appreciably. The consequent jet of steam into the fire was intended to cause such a disturbance that the fireman was bound to notice and to realise that the boiler needed more water. This was not always effective as the jet might make such a small difference to a big fire that the fireman was not alarmed into action. This led to a fatality at Lamington (between Glasgow and Carlisle) on 7 March 1948. The engine-men and three other men called in to investigate had heard a sound of escaping steam but none suspected that the fusible plugs had melted, and some time later there was a partial collapse of the fire-box as the result of overheating due to 'low water'. The official report criticised several members of shed staff for imperfection in their handling of a situation that raised doubts about the reliability of the gauge-glass indications, but said nothing about the inadequacy of the fusible plugs.

An alternative means (used in America but not in Great Britain) of drawing attention to a dangerously low water level in the boiler was the use of a float to blow a special whistle. A number of fatal boiler explosions were shown, however, to have occurred after whistles had correctly sounded but had been ignored. Temperament and tradition were factors in situations of this sort. Boiler explosions after about 1850 were not frequent occurrences, but their incidence per locomotive in service was always much lower (for example) in Great Britain than in America.

SUPERHEATING

After the injector, the only generally adopted addition to the Stephenson type of locomotive boiler was the superheater. This development took place the early years of the twentieth century, although superheaters had been in tried on locomotives at least as far back as the year 1852.

Given the slightest chance, steam taken from a boiler begins to condense back into the form of water. Any drop in temperature such as occurs when steam expands in pushing a piston into a cylinder causes condensation of some of the steam. Steam taken fom a boiler and raised by extra heat to a higher temperature without rise in pressure is said to be 'superheated'. From that condition it may be cooled (by expansion or otherwise) by a certain amount before condensation begins. It was discovered by trial that by superheating steam sufficiently to prohibit condensation in spite of cooling by expansion in the engine cylinders, coal consumption per unit of work done could be 20 to 25 per cent. less than when unsuperheated steam was used. No one strongly disputes this, although no one has produced a universally-accepted explanation of it.

Basic principles of physics suggest that if a steam locomotive be worked in academically perfect conditions a small additional economy might be achieved by superheating the steam to a higher temperature than suffices to eliminate condensation in the cylinder. The operating results of locomotives working in ordinary service conditions are in accordance with this suggestion to the extent that the small additional economy from what may be conveniently termed super-superheat is so small that it has never been clearly distinguishable in any practical test. Disadvantages of very hot steam are

1 a reduction in efficiency of the boiler/superheater combination; and

2 increased risk of trouble with cylinder-lubrication.

A sometimes useful advantage is a small saving in water.

A superheater is a complicated addition to the conventional Stephenson boiler and any leak of steam from any of its numerous pipe-joints can drastically spoil the 'steaming' of the engine by interfering with the draught in the smokebox, but on the whole it was worth having and it became accepted as normal equipment of a steam locomotive from about 1910.

A superheater 'element' is a long multiple coil of pipe in a fire tube specially enlarged to about $5\frac{1}{2}$ in. diameter to accommodate it. The number (perhaps 12 to 30) and dimensions of the elements are selected to give the desired degree of superheat to the steam. A superheater may be designed to give adequate but not excessive superheat in good working conditions. A bigger superheater than this may be used to give more than adequate superheat in the hope that it may be adequate even when flues are partially choked with cinders. Superheaters appreciably bigger still have been tried and have confirmed the expectation that their extra size offers no perceptible advantage.

THERMIC SYPHON

A device very little used in Britain, but included in the world-record-breaking boilers of the Chapelon 4C/4–8–0s on the Paris–Orleans Railway, was the 'thermic syphon' (see Fig. 7, p. 31). This was a central longitudinal partition about six inches wide in the upper part of the fire-box; it was tapered down into the form of a pipe by which it was fed with water from the underside of the boiler barrel. Convection produced a strong upward flow of water to the crown-sheet of the fire-box through the syphon.

It was a serious complication in constructing the fire-box and its operational advantage was distinguished only when the fire was being urged to exceptionally high temperatures by very strong draught. It was probably a vital factor in enabling the Chapelon boiler to maintain a reasonably high efficiency even when being urged to produce some 50 per cent. more steam than would normally be expected from that size of boiler. It did not, however, show any marked advantage in a Southern Region Pacific when worked hard on the British Railways test-plant at Rugby.

FRONT END

This is a convenient name, of American origin, for a locomotive's smoke-box and its contents. Its primary purpose is to exert on the fire a draught roughly proportional to the rate of discharge of steam from the blast pipe. It also serves, in some degree, as a receptacle for half-burnt coal that is lifted by draught from the fire and brought forward through the tubes. (In the popular literature of the locomotive, the term 'front end' is sometimes used with convenient vagueness to mean anything near to the front end of a locomotive, so that the reader becomes baffled or at best uninformed.)

Steam exhausted from the cylinders blows up from the blast-pipe into the chimney, drags with it the gases from the fire and shoots them out far faster than they would be moved by natural draught. This is necessary because in order to get worthwhile power from a locomotive boiler the fire must be worked at something like white heat, attainable only by strong draught. Gas in the smoke-box, in the tubes and in the fire-box must be at less than atmospheric pressure so that air is drawn briskly into the smoke-box from the ash pan through the fire-bed, the fire-box and the fire-tubes.

Through any leak in the smokebox, air enters and diminishes the draught on the fire. When the fire-door is opened while the engine is working, air rushes in, cooling the gases above the fire-bed and reducing the pull of draught through it, and so addition of coal to a fire is bound to cool it for a time. When no steam is issuing from the blast-pipe, the draught on the fire is small and flames may issue from the fire-hole to the danger of the engine-men. To avoid this, steam may be directed from the boiler to a small auxiliary multi-jet blast-pipe called the 'blower' (sometimes the 'jet') to produce enough draught to keep the flames going the right way. The chimney was sometimes made in several pieces and it was possible, though very unusual, for one of them to drop on to the blast-pipe in such a way as to direct the steam flow into the tubes and thus to blow a devouring flame through the fire-hole into the cab, with almost certain death for the engine-men. This was an example of the kind of thing the railway authorities had in mind when insisting on a signed indemnity from any non-official who was being specially permitted to ride on a working locomotive.

A vital necessity in every steam-locomotive was to design the front end so that the draught necessary to produce any required rate of combustion in the firebox could be produced by allowing the steam generated by the heat of that combustion to pass through the blast-pipe and the chimney into the atmosphere. A boiler and front end designed in this way was said to be 'draughted' for that particular combustion-rate. It meant that when working the engine at that rate, steam was produced as fast as it was used, and the boiler pressure would remain constant at or near the figure for which the safety-valves were set to 'blow-off', i.e. to permit some escape of steam. The engine was then said to be 'steaming' properly and this removed the engine-men's commonest cause for anxiety. What many students of the locomotive never did appreciate is that nothing that was done with the steam in passing from the boiler to the blast-pipe could prevent the engine from being made to 'steam' by appropriate adjustment of the blast-pipe. A common view that an engine could be prevented from steaming by cylinders that were too big or too numerous was entirely unfounded.

Some basic truths about front-end performance were re-affirmed and others established by Professor W. F. M. Goss after methodical experiments carried out at Purdue University (La Fayette, Indiana) in 1904. The results were reported to the American Railway Master Mechanics Association Committee on Front Ends. It is not known whether they were published but they were used in devising the American Master Mechanics' rules for guidance in front-end design. These could have been profitably used by some British designers long before they actually did, but even so it had to be accepted that some adjustment of dimensions on the basis of trial and error was usually required in arriving at the best front end for each design of locomotive and its class of service. The easily visible novelty of the American front end in Great Britain was the extension of the smokebox ahead of the chimney. Some onlookers denounced it as ugly, while to others it gave to the locomotive an aspect of energetic purpose sadly lacking in its flat-chested predecessors.

If conditions in the fire-box, tubes or smoke-box deteriorated, then any engine might not steam properly; this meant that if boiler pressure could be kept constant at all it might be much below the blowing-off point. Every engine-man knew that if any engine would not steam with careful firing, a sure remedy was to restrict the blast-pipe orifice by fixing a piece of metal across it. Through the reduced area, the steam had to come faster and so created a stronger draught. But authority forbade engine-men to use such restrictors on the ground that the back-pressure created by them had the effect of increasing coal consumption. This was absolutely correct but quite dishonest because the increase was negligible compared with the confidence that good steaming gave to the engine-men and it was they who had the responsibility of keeping the trains running.

Another factor in the situation was that the Drawing Office would never admit that any departure from the formal dimensions of a locomotive could be anything but disadvantageous. Officially, not the works, nor the shed-staff, nor the engine-men nor anyone else was allowed to deviate in any way from what was laid down on the manufacturing drawings. In actual fact, such deviations were common enough but not officially recorded.

The draught on the fire of a hard-working locomotive was commonly strong enough to lift cinders of anything up to $\frac{1}{2}$ in. in diameter to the roof of the fire-box, and thence through the tubes to the smoke-box. Any such cinder that happened to fly from a tube into the jet of steam from the blast-pipe was likely to be blown high into the air and then fall on to the train or the ground in its vicinity. If it happened to rest on anything combustible, a fire might be started as even after its aerial flight the cinder could be red-hot. At night many locomotives could be seen to be 'throwing sparks'. This was putting it mildly, as a half-inch cinder is heavier and more incendiary than a mere spark and at certain seasons of the year there could be considerable claims made on railway companies in respect of crops damaged by fire originated by 'sparks' from locomotives.

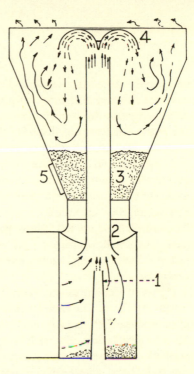

Fig. 10. Diamond stack that retains sparks ejected from smoke-box

To reduce nuisance and expense of this kind, locomotives were sometimes fitted with spark-arresting devices of one kind or another. Wire-netting bent into cylindrical form and mounted in the smoke-box between the blast-pipe and the chimney could keep the bigger sparks from getting into the chimney but its resistance to flow of gas could markedly reduce the draught on the fire especially when any considerable proportion of the wire-bounded rectangles have become blocked with cinders that entered but would not pass through.

The foregoing remarks on sparks apply to locomotives burning coal as was the common practice, but in some countries and especially in the early days of railways, wood was burned in steam-locomotives; it was common in many parts of America until about 1880. Some varieties of wood were apt to produce sparks in great profusion, and to cope with this, spark-arresting devices were developed and tried in fantastic forms and variety. The one well-known survivor was the 'diamond stack' (Fig. 10, above) that worked on a principle tried as far back as 1831. Over the top of the chimney (2) was a toroidal baffle (4) that directed the outflow vertically downwards on the outside of the chimney but inside a conical vessel that caught the sparks (3) while the gases rose once more and escaped gently through the annular space outside the baffle. The diamond stack, because of its necessarily large size, was hideous in the extreme but it was perhaps the simplest effective collector of sparks from fires in steam-locomotive engines. What very few illustrations make clear is that the diamond stack had near the bottom at least one door (5) that could be opened to allow the accumulated residue of large sparks to be extracted for disposal.

Long after the end of wood-burning in American locomotives, arose the practice of placing in the smoke-box a steel sheet or sheets formed so as to direct gases and sparks from the tubes into the lower half of the smoke-box which was extended ahead of the blast-pipe to form a resting place into which cinders fell while gas went up and was pulled back by the draught into the chimney. Cinders were filtered from gas, not by netting, but by their inertia which prevented them from making a quick turn upwards.

Plates in the smoke-box could thus arrest sparks without imposing too much restriction on the draught, but they were a nuisance because they hindered the periodically necessary operation of sweeping the fire-tubes. So this artifice was not widely used in Great Britain until some 30 years after its adoption as standard by the Great Western Railway round about the end of the nineteenth century.

It was found that when cinders (called 'char') had accumulated in the front of the smoke-box to such a depth as to interfere with gas-flow there, the smaller particles were picked up by the draught and did get thrown out of the chimney after all. But these were small, not very hot cinders that could not start a fire and it occurred to someone that as these cinders were thus not specially harmful, throwing them out of the chimney was a good way of getting rid of them. So arose the 'self-cleaning smoke-box' which came with that name from America to Britain during World War II.

It must be added, however, that virtually the same cleaning effect was achieved by at least one old British device, applied to all LNW locomotives after about 1880. When steam was directed into a perforated pipe in the bottom of the smoke-box it stirred up the char so violently that it was picked up by the draught to be shot out of the chimney and to fall on the coach roofs with a sharp pattering noise that the occupants were disposed to attribute to raindrops. By this means the fireman could 'clean' the smoke-box whenever and wherever he chose; he could, for example, apply it to discourage any urchin who looked as if he were about to drop a stone on to the engine from a bridge.

The self-cleaning smoke-box that came to Great Britain in the 1940s could not be controlled from the cab. It continuously ejected fine grit to fall as gentle rain from heaven upon the place beneath. It was liked by shed staff because it eliminated one of their worst jobs, but not by engine-men (because it reduced the draught on the fire) or by those who lived near the lines on which the engine worked. It seems likely that laws could have been invoked to prohibit the use of any device specifically designed to throw refuse into positions from which it was likely to fall on to property not owned by the user of the locomotive, and perhaps some hush-money was paid on this account.

The self-cleaning smoke-box was embodied in the standard British locomotive built after 1950, but the plates and wire-netting were not always properly replaced after removal for tube sweeping, if there was anywhere else to hide them.

After the period of speculation and experiment in locomotive design had given way to one of reasonable stability, it could be concluded by clear thinking that in any particular locomotive the blast-pipe diameter that was best for working hard was not the best for working easily and that as many locomotives might have to do both at different times, there was a case for some device for changing the effective diameter of a blast-pipe, simply by moving a handle. This does not at first sight seem very easy, but the worst of it was that in the heat, dirt and scouring cinders of a smoke-box, only very simple and rugged mechanism could be expected to remain reliable for more than the proverbial five minutes.

It can be said at once that no single type of variable blast-pipe ever gained anything like universal acceptance. The MacAllan blast-pipe cap was mounted on a rod that extended across the smoke-box close to the top of the blast-pipe, but clear of the steam that came from it. When it was judged advantageous to use a smaller blast orifice, the rod was rotated (by a crank linked to a lever in the cab) to turn the cap through a right angle and to place it firmly on the fixed blast nozzle. The device was an official mechanised version of the engine-man's unofficial restrictor. It had to be clearly understood that movement of the cap whilst steam was coming from the blast pipe was highly dangerous because during transition the cap might direct steam into the tubes and then flames would be forced into the cab even past the edges of a 'closed' fire-door.

The Great Western Railway made extensive use of the 'jumper-top' blast-pipe. In this, the normal circular orifice was supplemented by an annular one encircling it, except when the steam pressure at the nozzle was insufficient to sustain the weight of the 'jumper ring' which then dropped to cover the annulus. An unofficial restrictor for the jumper-top blast-pipe was most conveniently in the form of three steel wedges that could hold it permanently down regardless of steam pressure at the nozzle. It must have been difficult at any time to prove an advantage in use of the jumper top and always impossible to be certain at any moment whether the ring was up or down in designed accordance with the current value of the blast-pipe pressure. It was not retained in Great Western front ends re-designed to meet operating conditions after nationalisation of British railways in 1948.

The general aim in design of the front end is to attain the minimum blast-pipe pressure that will cause the issuing steam to pull air through the fire fast enough to maintain the combustion rate needed to maintain the required evaporation rate. For any particular combination of quantities and boiler dimensions, there is an ideal nozzle diameter and an ideal distance from the nozzle to the top of the chimney. The bigger the power output of the locomotive, the greater the ideal distance; if it exceeds the height available between the tops of the steam-chests and the undersides of tunnels and bridges, then the ideal condition is unattainable with a single blast-pipe.

But if two blast-pipes be used, each has to handle only half the output of the locomotive and the ideal height for that smaller power may be within the available height. This is the justification for using double blast-pipes and chimneys; for very high power, even triple chimneys might be justified. There is neither harm nor advantage in subdividing the steam flow into more numerous jets, or in jets of non-circular cross-sectional form.

As conventional steam-locomotives could work at high combustion rates with blast-pipe pressure not exceeding 5 lb. per sq. in. above atmosphere, there was clearly not much scope for great economy by using double blast-pipes. Reduction of back pressure by (say) 2 lb per sq. in. gave greater advantage when the mean effective pressure in the cylinders was low (i.e. at high speed) than when the engine was working hard at low speed. A front end designed for highest efficiency at high power output could be troublesome at low output and on that account multiple-jet blast-pipes were specifically excluded from British Railways standard designs.

It was sometimes found that a locomotive could develop much more power after having been fitted with a double blast-pipe than it did with its original single blast-pipe and that the difference was more than could be explained by the reduction in back pressure. An explanation is that as engine-drivers normally judged a locomotive's effort by the sound of the exhaust, the gentler discharge of the double blast-pipe induced them to work the engine harder than they would otherwise have deemed sensible

a. GC Director class 4–4–0 No. 506

b. LA No. 302 of the typical nineteenth-century American design

c. SR School class 4–4–0 No. 930 with multiple jet blast-pipe

d. GW County class 4–4–0 No. 3818

Plate 3

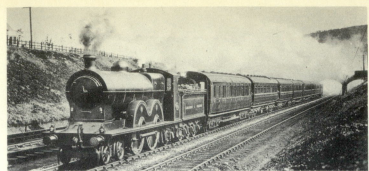

a. LY 4–4–2 No. 1424 with Leeds-Liverpool express near Mytholmroyd

b. GN 'Large Atlantic' No. 1421

c. Chicago & Eastern Illinois 4–4–2 No. 325

d. GC 4–4–2 No. 1086 with restaurant-car express near Wembley Hill

Plate 4

and, similarly, firemen would use fires of depth nearer to the ideal than they would have done with a stronger-sounding blast. Firemen could not help noticing that double-chimney engines were apt to burn a lot of coal, although the consumption was not necessarily unduly high in relation to the work done by the engine.

When locomotives became so large that chimneys had to be very short to clear the bridges, exhaust steam could be caught in the vortices of air formed behind the front edge of the smoke-box and might consequently tend to go down instead of up and so obstruct the driver's view of the road ahead. Plates and baffles in wide variety were mounted on and near the smoke-box with the intention of eliminating this difficulty. The most successful devices offered resistance to lateral flow of air from the front of the smoke-box and thus induced an upward trend. Smoke-lifting plates became common on large fast locomotives after about 1930 but the Great Western, for example, never found any need for them.

3
MECHANISM

THOSE who saw steam locomotives in their later days on British Railways are familiar with the mechanism formed (Fig. 1, pp. 8-9) by a rotating crank-pin (28), a connecting rod (32), a crosshead (34), moving between slide-bars (33) and connected by a rod (36) to something inside a cylinder (39). The invisible 'something' was a piston (38) closely fitting the circular interior of the cylinder. It was pushed alternately in opposite directions by steam admitted into the cylinder-ends and out of them by a valve (40) moved backwards and forwards by mechanism called valve-gear.

The exact position of the single cylinder of Trevithick's pioneer loco-motive (Fig. 2, p. 17) is uncertain but there is no doubt that it was hori-zontal for the crosshead slid on a horizontal rod projecting well ahead of the boiler to accommodate the 4-feet stroke of the piston and the crosshead. There were two identical connecting rods working cranks on the ends of a cross-shaft in the narrow space between the chimney and the rear end of the boiler. From this shaft the drive was conveyed to the nearer pair of the engine's four track-wheels by a train of three spur gear wheels. Many years later, the conventional 'steam roller' for flattening newly-made roads had a geared connection between its high crankshaft and its driving wheels, but when steam on rails had advanced beyond the single-cylinder design, gears were superfluous and undesirable.

Although all the stationary steam engines (mostly used for working mine-pumps) of his time had vertical cylinders, Trevithick discerned that on a horizontally moving locomotive a horizontally moving piston might be more appropriate and he built his locomotive accordingly. Nevertheless, most other steam locomotives for a quarter-century after Trevithick's leader had vertical cylinders in perpetuation of pumping practice. In the *Rocket* the Stephensons had moved the cylinders markedly from the vertical towards the horizontal, but it was left for Edward Bury to get right back to horizontal mounting for his inside cylinders working with a crank axle; the Stephensons afterwards used this construction for many locomotives.

During this period, however, the *Rocket* was rebuilt with its (outside) cylinders nearly horizontal, but not at the right end of the engine to enable it to be described as the first locomotive to have the mechanical layout of the ultimately preferred form.

In every early steam locomotive each valve was usually given its reciprocating motion by the particular type of crank known as an 'eccentric' mounted on the driving axle. There was one eccentric for each of the two directions of motion and the driver's operation of 'reversing' the engine meant breaking the connection between one eccentric and each valve and making a connection between the other eccentric and that valve. This sounds laborious and so it was until mechanism had been developed to facilitate it. One of these was the 'gab motion' in which each eccentric was connected by a rod to a V-shaped member or 'gab' which consequently had continuous backward and forward motion so long as the engine was running. The gabs faced each other over an intervening space in which lay a pin fixed in the valve spindle. One gab could be lowered on to this pin which was consequently guided to the point of the V and partook of its horizontal motion when the engine was running; in this way the valve was given motion appropriate for forward running. Raising the top gab out of contact with the pin was followed by raising the bottom gab into contact with the pin which could then be moved by the other eccentric appropriately for backward running.

LINK-MOTION

After some six years' use of gab motion, it occurred to one of the Stephensons' draughtsmen, named Williams, that the two gabs might be combined in the form of a single link with a parallel slot that, on reversing the engine, would convey the valve-spindle pin to its new position just as effectively as did separate gabs. Inexplicably he imagined this link to be applied to the eccentrics themselves whereas gabs had always been at the ends of rods worked by the eccentrics. It was left for Howe (another Stephenson employee) to realise, what now seems obvious, that the link would need to connect the eccentric-rods where the gabs were normally placed. So it seems reasonable to ascribe the invention of this 'link motion' to Williams and Howe, whereas it is usually called 'Stephenson valve-gear' because it was evolved in the Stephenson works. This is entirely misleading as inventions are normally credited to inventors and not to firms. It is quite certain that no one named Stephenson had anything to do with the invention of what is commonly called 'Stephenson valve-gear' or 'link-motion'.

When the use of link-motion had made the operation of reversing easy, it was found (by whom, it is not known) that if an engine was 'reversed' while running forward, hot gas in the smoke-box was drawn into the cylinders through the blast-pipe and the piston tried to push it into the boiler. One result was a braking effect on the train and many years later F W Webb on the LNW affected to set great store by it.

If, in a less dramatic form of this procedure, the link were moved from the full forward-gear position through less than half of its full displacement to full backward-gear, the engine continued to pull forward but less strongly. In this condition the valve-travel was reduced, less steam was admitted to each cylinder-end in each stroke, but it was used more effectively because while expanding behind the moving piston it continued to push it. Even with the mechanism set in mid-gear, i.e. halfway between full forward and full backward-gear, the engine continued to pull gently in the direction of motion (whichever it was) that immediately preceded the move to mid-gear.

It was realised after some study that running in full-gear gave a big pull but used steam wastefully, while running in positions between full-gear and mid-gear saved more in steam than it lost in pull. In short, the link-motion, and indeed any other that afforded gradual transition from full forward-gear to full backward-gear, enabled steam to be used expansively whenever the train could be hauled by less tractive effort than full-gear working produced.

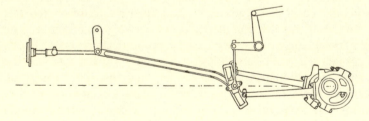

*Fig. 11. Stephenson valve-gear as applied
to a valve above the cylinder*

For some 60 years the link-motion was the most widely used type. With it went the type of slide-valve devised by Murray in 1806 to be the favourite for nearly a century. In the meantime the piston-valve had been invented and the Stephensons saw some of its advantages in the 1830s, but it was only when superheated steam created for slide-valves some lubrication difficulties less seriously suffered by piston-valves that the latter became generally accepted as preferable and indeed essential. Not that piston-valves were free from trouble, one of their defects being that in their original form with a single wide ring in each head, wear of the ring and of the cylindrical liner in which it slid could lead to such leakage of steam in fifty thousand miles of service as nearly to double the consumption of coal. It had been shown at least as far back as 1911, by Knorr in Germany, that this bad fault was avoidable by providing each head with a number of narrow rings of the type commonly used in pistons since the 1850s, but 20 years elapsed before any use was made of this knowledge in Britain.

OTHER VALVE-GEARS

The link-motion was invented in 1842 and two years later Egide Walschaerts working in Belgium produced a valve-gear of entirely different conception that did all that the Stephenson gear could do. Although more complicated for valves between the cylinders, the Walschaerts gear was superior to the combination of inside Stephenson gear and rocking-levers to drive valves over outside cylinders, and in the twentieth century this gradually came to be generally acknowledged.

Walschaerts valve-gear (*see* Fig. 1) was not properly appreciated in the United States of America till the twentieth century was a few years old, but soon afterwards it was accepted as normal for new construction. By 1914 it had appeared in a modified form known as the Baker valve-gear in which the slotted link and radius rod were replaced by an ingenious linkage not at all easy to explain in few words, but see Appendix 1.

In 1879 appeared the Joy gear, admirable in requiring no eccentric and in being directly applicable to a valve above the cylinder. It derived its motion from the connecting rod which was naturally apt to fracture if it were not made strong enough to take the extra loads imposed on it by the valve gear. It was used by the LNW and LY Railways in some 4,000 locomotives in Great Britain but it did not achieve comparable acceptance on locomotives elsewhere.

Development of the internal-combustion engine during the latter part of the nineteenth century had shown that it was practicable to control the movements of gas into a cylinder and out of it by a pair of poppet-valves opened by cams and closed by springs. Once the complication of camshaft, means of rotating it, and adjustable cams had been accepted, this arrangement might be applied to steam engines with the superficial advantage that at the design stage, the 'timing' of inlet and exhaust might be selected without restraint of inter-dependence imposed by the conventional flat-valve or piston-valve. This advantage is found on examination to be very small because what the ordinary valve permits is not bad, and although throughout the last 60 years of steam there was always someone, somewhere, trying poppet-valves in steam locomotives, flat valves or piston-valves worked by ordinary valve-gear were to be found in all but a very small percentage of steam locomotives. Poppet-valves can work with less power and less maintenance than piston-valves, but as even these do not require much of either, they leave no scope for marked improvement.

In too many places one may read expressions of opinion that one type of valve-gear gave high acceleration, another was best for high speeds, another wasted coal, and so on. This is pure illusion, as any of the accepted types of valve-gear could be designed to give valve-movements practically identical with those produced by any other type of gear. Where commentators went wrong was in unconsciously assuming that a comparison between a particular example of one type of gear and a particular example of another type was representative of every possible comparison.

Very late in the history of the steam locomotive it was realised that the gains to be realised from 'advanced' forms of valves and valve-gear were small compared with that obtainable from minimising leakage of steam past valves, pistons and glands. Defects in the last-named were unlikely to be overlooked, because steam that escaped past them into the open air was often easily visible and for a long time engine-drivers were responsible for keeping glands properly 'packed'.

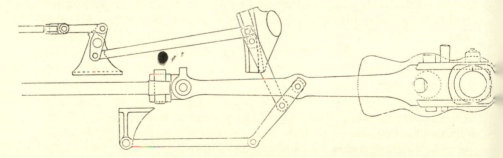

Fig. 12. Joy valve-gear, as applied on many LNW locomotives, with rocking-lever connection to the valve

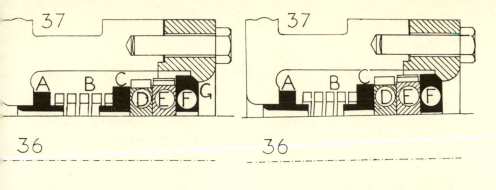

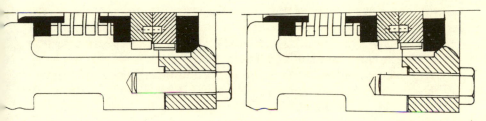

Fig. 13. Gland with spring-loaded metallic packing:

(left) *with everything in good order*   (right) *with wear of the crosshead allowing it to be above its original position*

PISTON-ROD PACKING GLAND

Like most other machines, the steam locomotive had a number of unobtrusive details that were vital to its performance and the gland or stuffing box was one of them. It encircles a piston rod where it passes through an end-cover of a cylinder. The rod must be gripped sufficiently tightly to keep steam-leakage down to a negligible amount, but not so tightly as to impose perceptible resistance to the motion of the rod. The common artifice in the early days of the steam engine was to wrap a rope of hemp round the rod in a multi-layered helix and then to squeeze it into tighter contact with the rod by axial pressure exerted by two nuts and bolts and by an annular plug. In favourable circumstances, including frequent readjustment, this worked satisfactorily, but when superheated steam was used, the higher temperature shortened the life of the rope and something else became necessary. So metallic packing was introduced and this had to simulate the flexibility of the hemp packing in accommodating errors in position of the piston-rod. One form of such packing is shown in Fig. 13.

Each of the components D and E is a ring made in overlapping halves, held fairly tightly on to the piston-rod (36) by C-shaped rings partly circling them. The component F is a bronze ring spherically formed at the right-hand outer edge to bear on a similarly formed recess in the end cover (G).

A helical spring (B) encircles the piston-rod and presses axially on a bronze ring (C) and so holds D, E, F and G in loaded contact. Because the flat surfaces are finely finished, leakage of steam between them is of negligibly small amount. Because E can slide easily on F, and because there is clearance between the piston-rod and the ring (F), the rod may move away from its central position (left) to conform to wear of the piston, crosshead or slide-bar and any tilt of the rod in relation to its normal direction is accommodated by sliding of F on its spherical seating in G. An extreme condition is shown in Fig. 13 (right).

The oblique position of the rod does not introduce any loss of contact on the flat surfaces of the rings and the gland is equally steam-tight in all positions. So the combination of D, E, F and G forms a seal that accommodates itself to quite considerable displacement of the piston-rod from the central position that it occupies when everything is right.

COMPOUND EXPANSION

Steam pressure in the boiler of the Trevithick locomotive was 40 lb per sq. in. and in the *Rocket* 25 years later was 50 lb per sq. in. Later advances made a boiler pressure of 100 lb per sq. in. fairly common by 1850. Steam exhausted from the cylinders of such locomotives might still be at 40 lb per sq. in. and it was natural to consider whether it might usefully be directed into another cylinder and do more work on a piston there. This would mean expansion in two successive stages, or 'compound expansion'. There was nothing new in this idea; indeed a patent in connection with it had been granted to Hornblower in 1781 and a compound engine had been built and tried in 1782 in conjunction with a condenser as was common practice in stationary steam engines.

Locomotives did not normally have condensers, but exhausted to to atmosphere and the difference of about 14 lb per. sq. in. restricted the possible advantage of compounding in locomotives. A result was that while condensers and compounding justified themselves to the extent that they were universally applied to stationary engines and to marine engines, compounding in steam locomotives never convincingly justified itself. A common misconception is that compound expansion must be greater expansion, whereas the restricted space for cylinders in a locomotive meant that a high expansion-ratio was less readily attainable with compound expansion than with single-stage expansion.

Nicholson on the Eastern Counties Railway built a compound locomotive in 1852, but nothing came of it. Between 1879 and 1902, F. W. Webb on the LNW built hundreds of compound locomotives and kept them in service despite their disadvantages. After his retirement his successor lost no time in scrapping the worst of them, although many of the others survived for 20 years or more.

It is not difficult to show on paper that unless steam were produced at a pressure of at least 800 lb per sq. in. (far above the practical limit for the Stephenson type of locomotive boiler) it was not practicable in a steam locomotive to expand steam usefully in the high ratio that was necessary for compounding to show any worthwhile economy over the best that could be achieved without it. So the coal-saving in actual practice could not be great, and to set against it was the extra cost, complication and maintenance of the compound engine. This was confirmed by numerous trials of compounding all over the world. The saving in total running cost was never more than marginal and as complication in a locomotive was always best avoided, most engineers decided that compounding was not worth pursuing. Here and there were 'pockets of resistance' as in France where some of the railways (but not all) were wholeheartedly in favour of compounding for 50 years or so, but when the French Railways were re-stocked with locomotives after World War II, it was not with compound locomotives.

In Great Britain, 3-cylinder compound 4–4–0s of a design that originated on the North Eastern Railway in 1898 were used on the Midland Railway and later on the LMS. They were 'successful' in that they were revered on the Midland and tolerated on the LMS but as they never numbered more than 240 out of over twenty thousand British locomotives, and as the much smaller group of other British compound engines gradually diminished after the Midland compounds reached their maximum, it is clear that compounding was not generally favoured in Britain although most railways had tried it.

In the 'W. M. Smith' system of compounding used in the Midland compounds, steam from the boiler passed (through the superheater on engines so provided) to the middle (high-pressure) cylinder, whence, after pushing the piston, half of it went to one outside cylinder and the other half to the other outside cylinder. The outside cranks were set at right angles and so the engine made four exhaust beats per revolution just as if it were an ordinary two-cylinder engine.

In starting from rest, the first movement of the regulator handle from the 'shut' position admitted steam to the steam chests of the outside (low-pressure) cylinders and the engine started as if it were an ordinary two-cylinder engine. In the starting condition the inside piston neither helped nor hindered as it had steam at a common pressure on both sides of it. Further movement of the regulator handle produced compound working by permitting steam from the boiler to pass to the high-pressure cylinder but not directly to the others.

In France, the favoured type of compound had two high-pressure cylinders and two low-pressure cylinders, but the most advanced French compound, built near the end of the steam era, had three cylinders on the W. M. Smith system.

Use was made in various places of compound engines, each with one high-pressure cylinder and one (larger) low-pressure cylinder. It is not known that any of these necessarily lop-sided locomotives achieved any distinction in performance. Those built by the North Eastern Railway in the late 1800s were rebuilt as conventional two-cylinder engines soon after their designer T. W. Worsdell had retired and had been succeeded by his brother, Wilson Worsdell.

Compounding was tried on locomotives in a wide variety of combinations and dispositions of cylinders, but it is impossible to give even elemental descriptions of them here without using more space than can be justifiably devoted to unsuccessful experiments. One can only express regret that so much effort should have been expended in striving for an object that could have been shown from the start to have at most only marginal advantage over the best attainable in the conventional steam locomotive.

A legend about compound locomotives is that their exhaust-noise was softer than that of a corresponding non-compound engine, but this does not withstand critical examination. The 'front-end' of every locomotive had to be designed, made and adjusted so that the blast was strong enough to make the boiler produce steam fast enough to pull the train and to keep the blast going. So unless the compound engine worked on much less coal than did the simple engine (and none ever did) its blast could not be markedly weaker than the weakest that sufficed in the corresponding non-compound engine. A difference could, however, arise where a compound engine was compared with a much smaller simple engine doing the same work. Such a comparison is weighted in favour of the larger engine and it is to be feared that this was a factor in some cases where appreciable economy was claimed for the compound. A fair comparison demanded, at least, a common boiler and equal nominal tractive efforts.

MORE THAN TWO CYLINDERS

A symmetrical compound engine had to have at least three cylinders and this was a justification for complicating an engine beyond the irreducible minimum of two cylinders. But even without compounding, a reason could be found for using more than two cylinders and the Stephensons built two 3-cylinder engines in accordance with an 1846 patent that they shared with Howe. They were different from 3-cylinder engines as normally understood in that the outside cranks were in line with each other and were at right angles to the inside crank. Each outside cylinder had only half the volume of the inside cylinder. In effect, one cylinder of an ordinary two-cylinder engine was divided into halves that were placed on opposite sides of the other cylinder. The object, successfully achieved, was that of preventing the out-of-balance forces on the reciprocating parts from producing any rocking action about either vertical or horizontal axes. This was an early example of 'balancing' but evidently the advantage from it was not great enough to justify the extra complication. In short, the ordinary two-cylinder engine was good enough at the time and so it continued for over a century. Nevertheless, large numbers of 3-cylinder and 4-cylinder engines worked over many years in Britain during the twentieth century and it was, mainly, the advantage of balancing that justified them.

With cranks at right angles, the reciprocating parts of a two-cylinder engine gave a backwards and forwards 'surge' in every revolution of the driving wheels, and its magnitude was proportional to the square of the speed. It could be offset by placing balance weights appropriately in the wheels, but the balance weights produced a vertical surge that exerted hammer blows on the wheels on the rail. In spite of this, balance weights were normally used and adjusted to reduce the horizontal surge by about half. By watching the motion of a balance weight in a wheel of a locomotive passing at speed, one might obtain a strong visual impression of the magnitude of its hammer blow on the track. At the ordinary top speeds of passenger trains the hammer blow could add more than 50 per cent. to the force exerted by the wheel on the rail. If the engine ran fast enough, the total force could be twice the weight on the wheel when the balance weight was at the bottom of its circular path and zero when the wheel had made half a turn.

By using four equal cylinders and setting the cranks appropriately, the horizontal forces produced by the two two-cylinder engines pretty well balanced each other and there was no need to 'balance' the reciprocating masses. Rather less satisfactorily, the same applied to 3-cylinder engines.

So 3-cylinder and 4-cylinder engines could be built to be light on the track and on the engine-men, but they were more expensive than the corresponding two-cylinder engines in both manufacture and maintenance and were therefore too expensive to be adopted as British Standards by British Railways after 1948. In America, objection to the cost and complication of extra cylinders was always very strong and very few American locomotives had more than two cylinders.

BRAKES

It is easy to understand that in the very early days of steam locomotives the problems of making them go and of keeping them going on nearly level track so uneven as to present plenty of resistance to running caused the subject of brakes to remain in the background. Each colliery vehicle normally had its own hand-brake and nothing more was needed.

But it is startling to realise that even when locomotives were able to haul passenger trains at over a mile a minute on main lines, no need had been felt to provide the engines with brakes. The Great Western broad-gauge singles, timed at 65 mph in the late 1840s, had no brakes; the six-wheel tenders had hand-operated brake-blocks on three wheels. Brake-men or 'guards' on the train could apply brakes to a few wheels when the engine-driver blew the whistle to call for that help. Forty years' extensive development of railways and acceleration of trains in Britain elapsed before Parliament enacted that every vehicle in every passenger train must have brakes operable by the engine-driver at all times, and automatically applied with full force should the train become divided by breakage of a coupling.

On the locomotive itself, steam was the obvious means of applying brakes without demanding much effort from the men and the Stephensons used it as early as 1832. It remained the normal power brake for locomotives during most of the nineteenth century but then some alternative use began to be made on locomotives of the type of power brakes (air or vacuum) applied on the passenger trains they worked. But always there was in addition, either on the engine or its tender, a hand-brake that, once applied, would remain 'on' without reliance on power of any kind until released by hand. Whenever a locomotive was to be left unattended, the hand-brake was applied, the valves set in mid-gear and the cylinder-cocks opened, so that no pressure could build up in the cylinders.

On the Webb locomotives of the London & North Western Railway, the piston in a steam-cylinder under the footplate moved a three-armed lever to pull backwards on the engine brakes and proportionally hard forwards on the tender brakes. This was economical in mechanism but had the disadvantage that the breakage of either pull-rod would leave both engine and tender without a power-brake. The scheme was discontinued on the North Western when Webb retired, but engines with brakes arranged in this way ran for many more years.

The vacuum brake is the last word in simplicity and reliability. Through-out the train extends the 'train-pipe'. Air is extracted from this by the 'ejector' on the engine, and in consequence from both ends of every 'brake-cylinder' in the train. In each cylinder is a piston and when there is no difference in air-pressure on the two sides of it, it is moved by its own weight and/or a spring to the position in which its piston rod holds the associated brakes 'off'. This is the condition for running the train. Admission of air to the train-pipe results in admission of air to the end of each cylinder occupied by its piston which is consequently moved by air pressure to apply the brakes. They are released by re-creating the vacuum in the train-pipe.

In the alternative system, air-brakes are released by pumping air into the train-pipe and thence into a reservoir associated with each brake-cylinder until the pressure in the pipe and the reservoirs is 90 lb per sq. in. In this condition a pressure-controlled 'triple valve' connects the brake-cylinder to atmosphere and the brakes are 'off'. Reduction of pressure in the train-pipe causes each triple-valve to admit air from its associated reservoir to the associated brake-cylinder and the brakes are applied with force proportional to the drop in train-pipe pressure. Although more complicated than vacuum-brakes, the air-brakes are equally reliable and are more quickly released. In both systems, many vehicles were fitted with 'quick-action' valves that reacted to any quick change in train-pipe pressure towards that of the atmosphere so as to augment that change.

Train brakes may be applied by opening a valve on the locomotive or in a guard's van, or (gently) by pulling a communication-cord in the train or (strongly) by division of the train by breakage of a coupling. Unless the locomotive is braked by the same method as the coaches, the change in train-pipe pressure moves a piston on the engine to make a roughly pro-portional application of its steam-brake or of its direct-acting air-brake.

It was common practice on steam locomotives to provide brakes for the coupled wheels but not (generally) for the other wheels. During the first decade of the twentieth century a number of British railways fitted brakes for bogie wheels but even the best combination of cylinders and levers in the small available space resulted in brakes that were more trouble than they were worth. Brakes on guiding wheels are moreover potentially dangerous in that when applied they impede the action of the springs in keeping the guiding wheels firmly in contact with the rails despite their irregularities.

Brake-blocks are preferably behind the wheels so that their radial pressure on them is in the opposite direction to the drag of the rails on them and so the pressure of axle-boxes on hornblocks is minimised. Convenience in siting brake-cylinders usually caused locomotive designers to place the brakes in front of engine-wheels and behind tender-wheels.

When a locomotive was running without steam it was usually being pushed by its train and because the opposite condition is a shade safer, brakes on locomotives were made weaker in relation to the weight than were brakes on passenger trains. A consequence was that a locomotive with a light passenger train was less easily stopped than it was with a heavy passenger train, but more easily stopped than it was with a goods train. For the greater part of British railway history most goods vehicles had no brake that could be applied while running at normal speed. Goods trains were checked only by the brakes on the engine and tender and by those applied by the guard to the 'brake-van' (weighing perhaps 20 tons) at the rear end of the train. Before going down a steep gradient a heavy goods train might stop in order to allow the guard to 'pin-down' the brakes on a number of wagons.

Leakage of air caused a vacuum-brake or a compressed-air brake slowly to diminish its grip on the wheels and so it was common to provide for permanent braking a hand-operated brake in each guard's van and on every locomotive or its tender.

UNDERCARRIAGE

Trevithick's pioneer steam locomotive had no frame or springs. Four feet attached to the underside of the boiler rested on axleboxes close to the four wheels that ran on the plateway. Others of the early locomotives were similarly primitive, but the jolts at rail-joints soon made it clear that springs were necessary and these were usually attached to a frame on which the boiler was carried. To accommodate the bouncing of the engine on its springs, each axlebox was left free to move vertically in the space between two guides called 'horns' (20) Fig. 1, and each pair of horns was tied together at the bottom by a 'hornstay'. The horns might form part of a structure called a 'bar-frame' or each pair might be united to form a horn-block attached to a 'plate-frame'.

Over all the later history of the steam locomotive, the bar-frame was the common construction in America, and the plate-frame in Britain.

Most locomotive springs were laminated, i.e. each formed as an assembly of long narrow plates, but use was also made of helical (coiled wire) springs and volute (spiral plate) springs. Laminated springs were expendable items and had to be examined regularly for broken plates. The weight on a spring was conveyed by it to an 'axlebox' (22) and so to an axle (23). In general, an axlebox was a block of metal with a semi-circular recess, lined with bronze on its underside. The bronze (or brass) was itself partially lined with 'white metal' which softens and eases the situation where and when local overloading of the sliding surfaces of the bronze and the axle is making things too hot. The sliding surfaces must be kept supplied with oil (a microscopic film suffices) as any failure produces overheating, and a burning-oil smell that warns the driver to take things easily and even to stop if he would avoid serious damage to the axlebox and the axle. Such a casualty is a 'hot box' and these were remarkably few considering that oil was delivered to many axleboxes at the worst possible place (on top), instead of underneath.

It is unusual for axleboxes and springs in a locomotive to be easily visible unless the frame-plates are outside the wheels (as they were under nearly all tenders) in which case they are admirably accessible. Nevertheless outside frames for locomotives passed out of favour because, requiring longer axles and longer cross-members than sufficed for inside frames, they made the engine unnecessarily heavy.

In the early days a plate-frame might be so 'skimpy' as to look from the side rather like a bar-frame, and even in the late 1800s some deep plate-frames were so extensively cut away as to give that same effect, but in general a plate-frame looked solid in a silhouette of a locomotive. By contrast, many bar-frames looked very light, but the bars were four or five inches wide whereas frame-plates were rarely so thick as $1\frac{1}{2}$ inches and so the former were laterally stiffer.

The earliest locomotives ran on four wheels, but George Stephenson had a six-wheeler running at Killingworth in 1815 and the majority of British locomotives over the whole life of steam on rails had six wheels.

As a locomotive could pull only by virtue of the frictional grip of its driving wheels on the rails, it was important that the propulsive effort of its pistons should be spread over as many wheels as were carrying enough total weight to prohibit slip on dry rails. This was best done by 'coupling-rods' applied to pins projecting from the bosses of the wheels at points with a quarter-turn displacement between the two wheels on each axle.

Coupling-rods could accommodate sideways movement of the wheels, up to an inch or so, relative to the frame, but not the larger lateral movements necessary to permit a long locomotive to pass round a sharp curve. For that purpose wheels at the ends of a long engine had to have more lateral freedom than coupling-rods could take and so only a fraction of the total weight of any such locomotive could be carried on coupled wheels. Every fast-running locomotive preferably had 'carrying wheels' at the front to ease its entry into curves and some of the larger ones also had carrying wheels at the back.

Although compelled by the coupling-rods to make identical numbers of revolutions, the tyres of coupled wheels always wore down to unequal diameters and this meant that even when running, as usual, with no apparent wheel-slip, they were 'scrabbling' on the rails and the coupling rods were constantly loaded in settling the fight between them. Because of this, early designers of high-speed locomotives preferred not to use coupling-rods but to rely on the driving effort that could be transmitted through a single pair of wheels. The power lost in friction associated with the coupling of wheels was difficult to measure but it had to be accepted where coupling of axles was necessary to obtain enough adhesion for the engine to do its job.

Because coupled wheels were not usually given the controlled sideways freedom necessary to guide the front of a locomotive smoothly round curves at speed, a locomotive without a pair of uncoupled wheels at the front was not ideal for regular fast running. It might well be able to run fast, but wear of the leading wheel-flanges and of the corresponding side-surfaces of the rail head would be excessive, even though the lateral flexibility of a plate-frame was beneficial. Use of the laterally stiffer bar-frame and of outside cylinders necessarily set further ahead of leading coupled wheels than inside cylinders might be, combined to limit American use of locomotives with leading driving wheels to low-speed switching (shunting) service. An extreme example of this was the Union Rail Road 0–10–2 'switching and transfer' locomotives (Ref. Z11) built by the Baldwin Locomotive Works in 1936; at a weight of 180 tons they exceeded every

a. LY superheater-fitted 2–4–2T. A long eight-wheeler

b. No. 44 of a LNW class introduced in 1906

c. Preserved member of LNW 'Coal Tank' class

d. One of a class of two LBS tank engines. The other had outside Walschaerts valve gear

Plate 5

a. Rebuilt form (1881) of the most numerous British class (DX of LNW)

b. Union Pacific RR 2/0–6–0 switcher

c. SR Class Q 0–6–0 (1938)

d. Typical small British shunting engine (NE design)

Plate 6

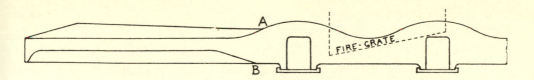

Fig. 14. *Plate-frame for a 4–4–0 locomotive. To the left of AB, the two inner lines represent the form of an outside frame that might be added to make a double frame. To the right of AB the outlines of the frames are identical.*

British 12-wheel locomotive by at least 60 per cent. and with 85 sq. ft. of grate area by at least 70 per cent. Axle loading of over 31 tons was 40 per cent. higher than anything permitted in Great Britain. In contrast may be mentioned the fifty 'Terrier' 0–6–0 tank engines built for the London, Brighton & South Coast Railway in 1872-80 and used for many years on short-distance passenger trains. The total loaded engine-weight was less than 28 tons, and the grate area 10 sq. ft.

A contrast between typical plate-frames and bar-frames for a 4–4–0 locomotive is shown in Figs. 14 and 15. Early bar-frames were built up by uniting wrought iron bars by welding and/or by bolting. The main members of plate-frames were produced by rolling wrought iron and the cross-members by forging. In later years forged steel replaced wrought iron, but a really momentous change came in the twentieth century when it became possible to make a whole bar-frame (or 'bed') as a single steel casting. Further development in the same direction enabled cylinders, smoke-box saddle and other components to be formed with the bed as a single piece of cast steel perhaps 50 ft. long. Only foundrymen can really appreciate the magnitude of this American achievement.

The alternating forces applied by steam-pressure to cylinders caused them to be constantly trying to detach themselves from the frame and the perennial problem of providing secure fastenings became intensified as

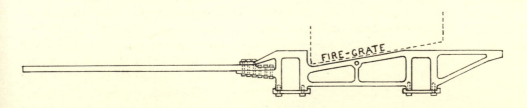

Fig. 15. *Bar-frame for a 4–4–0 locomotive. The slender extension on the left ties the main part of the frame to the underside of the combination of outside cylinders and smoke-box saddle.*

American locomotives grew bigger and bigger, until at a stroke it was eliminated by making cylinders and bed in one piece. Adoption of this construction made no perceptible difference to the appearance of a locomotive, nor to its performance as a power-producer, but it did reduce long-term maintenance costs.

On the Great Western Railway, double plate-frames predominated in the nineteenth century but new designs standardised shortly afterwards attached outside cylinders and smoke-box saddle to a short bar-frame extension ahead of a conventional plate-frame, and this persisted for over 40 years. In the early days of British Railways, bar-frames and cast-steel beds were considered but it was found that available resources could produce plate-frames at lower cost.

Where in any mechanism one member is to be continually sliding on another

1 the materials must be appropriate
2 the surfaces must be smoothly finished
3 a lubricant is necessary
4 dirt should be kept away.

In a steam locomotive (4) was usually impossible and (3) tended to be uncertain and in consequence wear had to be accepted as inevitable. So it was common to make sliding connections in such a way that re-adjustment could compensate for wear. At the ends of coupling-rods and connecting-rods were pairs of 'brasses' that were held by adjustable wedges to bear as lightly or as heavily as might be desired on the steel pin between them. Part of routine maintenance was to ascertain the clearance at each such bearing and to re-adjust the wedge accordingly. This had to be done carefully if the bearing were to run without overheating and the wedge were not to become loose in running.

Over a period of 30 years or so, improvement in materials, lubricants and protection against dirt made it possible to dispense with adjustability of some bearings. A single brass replaced the two adjustable pieces, and when it became excessively worn a new one was substituted for it. Ends of coupling-rods were simplified in this way in the nineteenth century, but 'solid big-ends' of connecting-rods did not appear in Great Britain until the Great Western adopted them in 1902. 'Big ends' on inside cranks had to be split to permit of assembly and were therefore easily made adjustable although that was not imperative.

A consequence of non-adjustability of brasses was that coupling-rods and connecting-rods with worn brasses were apt to make clanking noises when the engine was running in many combinations of speed, regulator opening and cut-off. Such noises were so common that one ceased to notice them. But when, as could happen in Germany for example even in the 1950s, one encountered a locomotive with very finely adjusted brasses, the absence of noise from its mechanism was very noticeable indeed.

WHEELS

Although critics periodically asserted that the steam locomotive never successfully departed in principle from the 1829 *Rocket*, no one pressed the point that all locomotives had circular wheels. Trevithick used circular wheels and 140 years later Lawford H. Fry mentioned in playful defence of locomotive engineers that the circle was still the best shape for wheels. The wheel as a mechanism is so simple compared with some other things in a locomotive that it is easily overlooked, but it does merit a little attention.

Normal practice was to make a locomotive-wheel by fitting a fairly hard steel ring or tyre to a 'wheel-centre'. Many early wheel-centres were built of cast-iron sectors carefully fitted and fastened together, but for 50 years or so, until steel castings became practicable for wheel-centres, each one was laboriously built up by welding wrought-iron spokes between a central boss and a ring where the spacing of the spokes was about nine inches. Cast steel was naturally adopted as a much less expensive alternative as soon as its reliability had been established. Much less expensive even than this was cast iron, employed by the LNW for wheels less than 5 ft in diameter in a design that compensated for the weakness of cast iron by using broad, H-section spokes at about 12-inch spacing at the wheel-rim. In the 1930s and afterwards some use was made of a design of cast-steel wheel in the form of two discs with internal radial ribs or with cross-stays in the form of open-ended tubes. None of these alternatives looked anything like so elegant as the conventional cast-steel wheel-centre with narrow spokes.

The wear of tyres was carefully watched as safe guidance of the locomotive by the rails depended on close adherence to the nominal profile of the wheel flanges. So tyres were repeatedly re-machined until it was decided that they were too thin to be safe; the diameter might then be as much as three inches less than that of the tyre when new.

RAILS

For by far the greater part of British railway history, the rails were carried in cast iron 'chairs' bolted down on to wooden sleepers and the rhythmic sound of the passage of coach wheels over rail-joints was a well-known characteristic of travel by rail. British rails were normally of the slightly unsymmetrical I-section known as 'bull-head' but most of the world's rails were of a sectional form that is much wider at the base than at the top and is identified as 'flat-bottom'. Such rails were commonly held down on the sleepers by spikes that served also to give lateral location but the flat-bottom rails of British Rail are clamped to cast-iron baseplates fixed to the sleepers.

Adjacent rails were commonly clamped together by bolts and 'fishplates' with a gap of about a quarter of an inch to allow for expansion of the rails in hot weather and the joints were periodically slackened, greased and re-tightened. Nevertheless the joint was often too tight to permit any expansion and so hot weather could subject the rails to compressive stress which produced a risk of lateral buckling. The lateral stiffness of flat-bottom rails reduces the risk of buckling to the extent of permitting them to be united by welding and this eliminates rail-joints, reducing noise and impact stress, but deprives the train-timing enthusiast of his most convenient method of measuring the speed of a train over a distance of the order of a mile. For rails are made pretty precisely to standard lengths and this enabled any observer to use his ears as a means of measuring the distance covered by the train during an interval of time known from unbroken observation of the hand of a watch.

Rails are made from some of the less expensive grades of steel with composition selected to provide a good compromise between softness and brittleness. Maximum permissible wheel loading in Britain is about eleven tons whereas as much as eighteen tons has been allowed in America. The difference is associated with the stronger, and therefore heavier, rails and the closer setting of American sleepers or, as they are called there, ties.

The springing of railway coaches is so 'soft' that the passenger is largely insulated from the effect of imperfections in the track over which he is carried. Engine-men had not the same protection as locomotive springs were necessarily pretty stiff; indeed one might ride on many steam locomotives and form the impression that they had no springs at all. But even the rails have some elasticity and a vivid impression of it can be obtained simply by watching a couple of adjacent sleepers under a moving train instead of looking at the train itself. Specially impressive is the deflection of rails at a rail-joint; observation of this was not to be recommended to any nervous person who might have to travel by train afterwards as the rail-depression might depress him to the point of alarm.

But any quick up and down movement is usually much smaller than it seems to be and what looks like several inches may in fact be less than half an inch. The elimination of joints and joint-impacts by use of continuously welded rails enabled maximum allowable axle-loads to be increased, but extensive use of continuous welding of rails came too late in Britain to affect steam-locomotive design.

WHEEL ARRANGEMENTS

A complete list of all the wheel arrangements ever used for steam locomotives from 2–2–0 to 4–8–8–4 is too long for inclusion here, but some specially named ones are mentioned below:

2–4–2	Columbia
4–4–0	American
4–4–2	Atlantic
2–6–0	Mogul
2–6–2	Prairie
4–6–0	Ten-wheeler
4–6–2	Pacific
4–6–4	Baltic or Hudson
2–8–0	Consolidation
2–8–4	Berkshire
4–8–0	Mastodon
4–8–2	Mountain
4–6–6–4	Challenger
2–6–6–6	Allegheny

In nearly every case the name arose out of some circumstance relatable to the building date of the first locomotive of the wheel-arrangement concerned, and has no technical significance whatever.

After the Whyte system had become well established, there was little purpose in devising names for wheel-arrangements and so the later ones (those of big locomotives) were little used. 'Challenger' sounds formidable, although slightly lacking in dignity, but 'Big Boy' is a regrettably trivial name for the gigantic Union Pacific 4–8–8–4s. The completion of the first of these engines was celebrated by a formal dinner at which someone referred to it as the greatest locomotive on earth. This was recognised as unfortunately appropriate when it was learned later that the engine was at the time derailed and setting a formidable problem to a breakdown gang.

Mention should be made of a 4–14–4 locomotive built at the Luyansk locomotive works in 1935 for hauling heavy coal trains in the USSR. The distance between the first and last coupled axles was 32 ft. and they probably had spring-controlled lateral movement. The three middle coupled wheels on each side had 7-inch wide tyres with no flanges. With axle loads limited to 20 tons, the weight of the locomotive could not have exceeded 220 tons, well surpassed by the 276 tons of the Pennsylvania 4–4–6–4s. It is believed that only one 14-coupled locomotive was ever made and so it may be judged that it was not a success.

A landmark in wheel-base development was the application of a four-wheel truck under the fire-box. It was a natural consequence of the need to provide bigger fire-boxes for the development of high power. It is hard to say which locomotive was the first to have a four-wheel trailing truck but it was a feature of a few experimental engines built for the Northern Railway of France a few years before World War I (e.g. 10b).

Serious adoption of the four-wheel trailing truck is usually associated with the Lima Locomotive Corporation which from 1925 'pushed' to American railroads the 2–8–4 as a locomotive for fast freight traffic. In 1927 the New York Central Rail Road used the same principle in its 4–6–4s for fast passenger trains and finally adopted the 4–8–4 wheel arrangement for that class of service. In the meantime, most American railroads had been compelled to build locomotives so big that use of a four-wheel trailing truck became natural, or indeed imperative. It never became similarly necessary in Great Britain and only one tender locomotive (LNER No. 10000) had two carrying axles at the rear end.

In a logical development of its former advocacy of the four-wheel trailing truck, the Lima Locomotive Corporation built for the Chesapeake & Ohio Rail Road in 1942 a number of 4-cylinder articulated locomotives with the wheel-arrangement 2–6–6–6. This was in effect the Lima's favourite 2–8–4 lengthened by 50 per cent. in each of its two main sections.

Although the largest locomotives running in Great Britain in, for instance 1960, were much larger than any in, say 1835, the majority of the stock were at all times six-wheelers. At the later date the six-wheelers were almost exclusively 6-coupled engines, i.e. 0–6–0s, and indeed for the greater part of the intervening period there were in Britain more 0–6–0s than locomotives of all other wheel-arrangements put together.

A Stephenson 0–6–0 had run at Killingworth in 1815, Hackworth built the *Royal George* 0–6–0 in 1827 and the Western Region of British Railways was building 0–6–0 tank engines as late as 1954. If weight of numbers were regarded as all-important, a review of British steam on rails could be confined to 0–6–0 tender engines and 0–6–0 tank engines.

This prevalence of a type of locomotive that was not good as a regular fast runner merely emphasises that a great deal of railway haulage in Britain was satisfactorily done at less than about 40 mph.

During the 25 years between the beginning of grouping (1923) and the beginning of nationalisation (1948) there were some considerable changes in British locomotive stock. Numbers of 4–6–0s and 2–6–0s were more than doubled, the number of 2–8–0s was multiplied by four, and the number of Pacifics rose from five to 279. The number of 2–6–2 tender engines changed from zero to 186, of which all but two were Gresley's LNE Class V2 closely comparable in the main dimensions with the A3 Pacifics. The total number of 0–6–0s went down rather noticeably from about 10400 to about 7400, although they still numbered 37 per cent. of the total of 20000 locomotives. This change was associated with the strengthening preference for outside cylinders as the years went by, and the consequent building of the 2/2–6–0 where the 0–6–0 would otherwise have been the natural choice.

Numbers of locomotives of various wheel arrangements on British Railways on 1 January 1948

Tender		Tank	
0-6-0	4,383	0-6-0	3,057
4-6-0	2,503	0-6-2	1,246
4-4-0	1,615	2-6-2	769
2-8-0	1,469	0-4-4	590
2-6-0	1,009	2-6-4	535
0-8-0	952	2-4-2	285
4-6-2	279	4-4-2	267
2-6-2	186	0-4-0	196
4-4-2	64	2-8-0	151
2-4-0	24	4-6-2	134
0-4-2	4	0-4-2	125
4-6-4	1	2-8-2	54
0-10-0	1	2-6-6-2	33
	———	0-8-0	22
Total	12,490	0-8-4	20
		4-8-0	17
		2-4-0	17
		0-8-2	10
		0-6-4	7
		2-8-8-2	1
		Total	7,536

ARTICULATED LOCOMOTIVES

Quite early in the history of the steam locomotive it was found useful to support the leading end by a four-wheel truck or bogie, rotatable relative to the bulk of the locomotive through a small angle about any axis. This made the locomotive able to accommodate itself more readily to curvature and other irregularities in the track. Because it is in effect two 4-wheel vehicles, a 4–4–0 locomotive (for example) may be said to be 'articulated' but in practice that term is reserved for a locomotive in which each of at least two frames connected by universal joints has cylinders and mechanism for applying driving effort to some of its wheels.

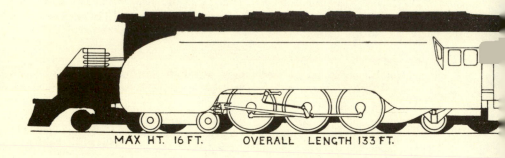

MAX HT. 16 FT.   OVERALL LENGTH 133 FT.

Fig. 16. Comparison between UP 4–8–8–4 (Ref. Z15), LMS Coronation Pacific (9d) and Rocket

In the early days of steam there were many variations on the basic principle and articulation in many forms was contemplated and in some cases actually tried in metal. The two forms that achieved considerable success in service were

1 that originated by Anatole Mallet in 1884 and originally applied with compound expansion of steam in four cylinders;
2 that originated by H W Garratt in 1912 and extensively developed by Beyer, Peacock & Co. (Manchester) in the 'Beyer-Garratt' locomotive.

The essential distinction between these forms of articulated locomotive is that in the Mallet locomotive the main part of the boiler is
mounted on the rear frame, while its leading end receives additional
support from the leading frame, which is hinged horizontally and vertically
to the rear frame.

In the Garratt locomotive the boiler is wholly mounted on a girder-frame
supported at each end by a 'power bogie' in the form of a conventional
locomotive frame with coupled wheels, cylinders and motion and in many
cases additional carrying wheels. Each power bogie can swivel in relation
to the main frame. A great advantage of this design is that there are no

wheels beneath the ashpan and so there is exceptional freedom in designing
the fire-box and ashpan.

The normal justification for building an articulated locomotive is an
unusually low ratio of the radius of the sharpest curve it must negotiate
to the minimum length it must have in order to impose on the track
sufficient weight to enable it to produce the required pull or push. As it
is pull, or push, rather than power that is the dominating factor, articulated
locomotives might be expected to be built for slow slogging rather than for
normal speeding and that was in fact generally the case before about the
year 1930. The largest locomotive ever to be used in Britain was the LNE

6/2–8–8–2 (Ref. 14d) built in 1925 and employed in 'banking' goods trains at low speed up the Wentworth incline between Worsborough (near Barnsley) and Penistone.

The only other Garratts used on British main lines were the 33 LMS 4/2–6–6–2s (Ref. Z10) mostly used on coal trains run between Toton (Long Eaton) and Cricklewood (North West London). Normal practice had been to double-head such trains with Midland 0–6–0s; one Garratt could replace two 0–6–0s and save two men's wages.

In the United States the four-cylinder compound Mallet appeared in 1903 in the form of a modest 0–6–6–0 (Ref. Z13) for the Baltimore & Ohio Rail Road, but in the ensuing 20 years designers fairly let themselves go. The outstanding example in this period was the Erie Rail Road 6C/2–8–8–8–2 'Triplex' locomotive (Ref. 14b) in the form of a Mallet 2–8–8–0 followed by a tender supported by a third set of eight-coupled wheels.

The high-pressure cylinders were the second pair and the exhaust from them was equally divided between the other two pairs. All pistons had 36 in. diameter and 32 in. stroke; 16-in. piston valves were worked by Baker valve-gear. Exhaust from the leading cylinder went up the chimney in the ordinary way; exhaust from the rear cylinders passed through pipes in the tender to warm the water and reached the atmosphere through a vertical pipe at the rear. Used for banking up steep gradients, these locomotives were successful enough to be kept in service for nearly 20 years.

A 4C/2–10–10–2 design of Mallet locomotive (Ref. Z16) for the Virginian Rail Road had low-pressure cylinders of the locomotive record-holding diameter of 48 in.

Some development of the Mallet-type locomotive as a vehicle had to take place before it was safe at passenger-train speeds, and before it could attain such speeds compound expansion had to be abandoned.

The non-compound articulated locomotive of the Mallet type was numerously introduced by the Chesapeake & Ohio Rail Road in 1924 and after that no more compound Mallets were built in America except by the Norfolk & Western Rail Road in 1948-52. The non-compound Mallets were, however, produced in considerable numbers and variety until 1945. By 1929 the Northern Pacific had 4/2–8–8–4s (Ref. Z14) weighing 320 tons each; the Union Pacific 4/4–8–8–4s (Ref. Z15) built in 1941-44 beat this substantially with 345 tons, and were followed by tenders weighing 194 tons each when fully loaded. Not only were these Union Pacific giants the world's largest and most powerful pullers but they could run safely at 80 mph.

An awkward feature of any articulated locomotive is the need to convey steam to and from cylinders on a frame that moves relatively to the boiler. It demands ball-and-socket type joints from which leakage of steam must not be allowed to exceed a very small amount in spite of considerable angular relative movement.

Of Garratt locomotives with two cylinders for each group of driving wheels, it was said that the exhaust beats from the two sets of cylinders automatically 'synchronised', i.e. that there were four per revolution of the driving wheels just as if the locomotive had only two cylinders. It was hard to imagine why this should be so, particularly as the two sets of wheels, because of inevitable differences in diameters, themselves were not 'synchronised'. It was eventually decided that the 'synchronism' of exhaust beats was a myth generated by imperfect observation and the tendency of the beats from the two cylinders nearest to the chimney to dominate the sound-pattern. The other beats were softened by the volume of the long pipe that conveyed them to the smoke-box.

4
FUEL, WATER, AND MAINTENANCE

FUEL

The earliest steam locomotives were associated with collieries and so they naturally burned coal; other fuels were used later but over the complete history of steam on rails, locomotives burned more coal than anything else. But although coal was the first and obvious choice as fuel for steam locomotives, it was soon abandoned because it made too much smoke. This might be tolerated in the immediate vicinity of collieries, but not when locomotives began to run into residential areas. The readily available, but more expensive, alternative was coke which was virtually smokeless, and smokelessness was one of the specific requirements imposed on the locomotive competitors in the Rainhill contest of 1829. They used coke and found it good in that it was reasonably clean to handle, could burn very hot and produced neither smoke nor harmful sparks, but it could cost nearly twice as much as coal and was more severely abrasive to fire-boxes and fire-tubes.

When heated, coal produces gases that are compounds of hydrogen and carbon, both combustible when in contact with oxygen at a sufficiently high temperature. If there is plenty of oxygen thoroughly mixed with the gas, then the hydrogen burns and produces superheated steam, while the carbon burns and produces carbon dioxide which is another invisible gas. But if there is insufficient oxygen to enable both the hydrogen and the carbon in a molecule of gas to burn, the hydrogen seizes what oxygen it needs and such carbon as fails to find oxygen for combustion is left as atoms of a black solid. Large numbers of atoms or collections of atoms of carbon, floating in the air, constitute a cloud of black smoke. To avoid production of such smoke is merely a matter of mixing enough oxygen with the gases immediately over the fire-bed or, in practice, of allowing air to be drawn into the fire-box in a way that ensures good mixing with hot gases rising from the fire-bed. This is simple enough now, but it was not so in the days before the elementary principles of chemistry had been recognised. Until enlightenment came, use was made of coke, which is coal deprived of its hydro-carbons by heating and is therefore carbon with no hydrogen to make prior claims on any oxygen that comes near.

For nearly 30 years coke continued as the conventional fuel for loco-motives, which when running without steam in darkness might trail from the chimney a beautiful blue flame of burning carbon monoxide. Neverthe-less many people strove to find a way of using less costly coal without producing offensive smoke. Many and complicated were the unsuccessful devices tried in this quest and most engineers may have abandoned it as hopeless when, relatively quickly, the problem was solved. In 1857, G R Griggs on the Boston & Providence Rail Road, placed a brick arch above the fire. In 1858, Douglas on the Birkenhead, Lancashire & Cheshire Junction Railway placed a deflector plate in the fire-box immediately above the fire-hole. In 1859, Charles Markham, working for Matthew Kirtley on the Midland Railway, applied arch and deflector plate at the same time, and with these and a bit of care by the fireman, most kinds of coal could be used without making a great deal of smoke.

So coal came back as the natural fuel for locomotives, at least in coal-producing countries. The alternative was wood, where it was obtainable in adequate quantities at lower cost than coal. This was the case in certain parts of North America until about 1880; after then the use of coal for locomotives was universal in that country for about a quarter of a century. In the south-western States, well away from coalfields, oil-burning had been tried and in the twentieth century became established practice on steam locomotives in those areas.

Except where indigenous wood was cheap and plentiful, steam loco-motives normally burned coal even though it had to be brought over long distances by sea. This was economical only because of the very low cost of long-distance transport by water. Once a big load has been placed on a ship, it can be moved at only about one-twentieth of the cost of carrying it by land. So although large quantities of locomotive coal were carried for hundreds and even thousands of miles overseas, within Great Britain a rail-way company could find it worthwhile to spread its purchases of coal over collieries in such locations as to minimise the total cost of carriage of coal to engine-sheds. Any running-shed might be supplied at any one time with different kinds of coal to be distributed to the locomotives according to their classes of work, i.e. passenger trains, goods trains and shunting.

Not all coal could be successfully burned in steam locomotives, and of the varieties that could, some were superior to others. To deal with coal that came in very small pieces, the designer's procedure was to provide the locomotive with a very much larger grate-area than would suffice for ordinary coal, so that the air-speed through the fire-bed was not high enough to lift coal from it at an excessive rate. That artifice was used in Belgium to handle rather poor coal and also at certain times and places in North America to deal with small anthracite, excellent as a fuel but in most other locations far too expensive for use in locomotives.

Although locomotive coal might be bought on the basis of calorific value, that was not its most important characteristic to the engine-men. What mattered to them was (1) absence of fusible ash that could produce clinker; and (2) presentation in lumps of convenient size. Handling of coal on the way from the coal-face to the engine-tender inevitably produced some dust and 'slack' which were hardly worth placing in the fire-box because the draught would take them straight up and into the smoke-box. Lumps bigger than about 12 inches cube had to be broken because they would not go through the fire-hole; lumps much bigger than that might block the way from the tender to the shovelling plate. Pieces of about six inches cube were ideal for firemen and occasionally some were supplied. Superficially identical coals from adjacent collieries might behave quite differently on the fire, and so a fireman's life could have plenty of variety besides, in many circumstances, a fair amount of hard labour.

Coals might be classified as hard or soft according to their reactions to blows from a coal-hammer; they could also be classified as bituminous, semi-bituminous or not bituminous, according to the length of flame that they produced. They also showed differences in rate of deterioration with storage time. Coal dropped on to the back of a tender might remain there for months or years. When it was at length brought forward in some difficult running conditions that had consumed all the coal from the readily accessible parts of the tender, its performance in the firebox might be very disappointing.

Coals commonly burned in steam locomotives were distinguishable primarily as 'long-flame' and 'short-flame', the variation in this respect being associated with the range (about 23 per cent. to 8 per cent.) of content of carbon combined with hydrogen in volatile carbon compounds in the coal. The range of content of carbon as such was about 62 to 84 per cent. 'Long-flame' coals would readily produce smoke unless the fireman took care; 'short-flame' coals were less troublesome in this respect. Anthracite (not normally burned in steam locomotives) could hardly be made to produce any smoke; coke produced none.

An interesting characteristic of some kinds of coal is the swelling that they undergo in the heat of a fire. Among British coals used in locomotives, it was most clearly demonstrated by most of the South Wales steam coals and engine-men were well aware of it. Such coals are low in volatile matter; this is the reason for their ability to be burned without producing much smoke and for their reluctance to be lit by anything but a hot fire. It was common practice with such coals to build a big fire gradually during the hour's preparation time of an engine before it left the shed for its day's work, and the swelling of the coal between the end of the build-up and complete incandescence could be very noticeable especially when it had gone so far as to prevent the fireman from opening a fire-door of the type that had to be swung into the fire-box for that purpose.

Swelling of coal was one of those phenomena that were never fully explained to the satisfaction of all critical experts. Its existence is, however, universally accepted and indeed to the extent that there is a recognised method of measuring the 'swelling index' of a coal. In the temperature range of about 350 to 450 degrees Centigrade a swelling coal changes from a hard brittle material to a soft plastic mass that is inflated into a froth by gas produced by chemical decomposition, and when that has been completed the remaining carbon becomes hard again in the cellular form recognised as coke. In that state it presents much more surface to air drawn through it by the draught on the fire than does non-swelling coal and has consequently a higher combustion-rate per cubic foot of coal in the fire. So a fireman used to Welsh coal could be disappointed even before a run began by his observation that the coal he had got was not swelling so much as he had reason to expect.

But discrimination of this sort was merely in standard of excellence. What was far more disconcerting was the degree of badness that might be attained by coal supplied to locomotives in the later days of steam.

The worst coals were those that produced clinker, which is ash that has melted in the full heat of the fire, has dropped into the less hot vicinity of the fire-bars and has there solidified into a cake that tends to cling to them. Molten ash lifted from the fire by the draught might strike the underside of the brick arch, cling to it, and build down to form incandescent stalactites. It could also be carried by draught to the tubes and gradually build up on the entrance to each one a ring (called a 'birdsnest' even in France) that obstructed the draught.

On a long run, clinker could gradually extend on the grate in a way that blocked most of the air-spaces and halved the power of the engine. A fireman might try to ease the situation by moving clinker into local heaps but it was an unrewarding task as the heat of the fire when the engine was pulling would make any fire-iron too soft to be of any use in about half a minute. Fire-cleaning, i.e. removal of clinker from the fire-box, was usually practicable only when the engine could remain stationary for a time long enough for the fire to become dull.

Fire-irons were bars long enough to reach to the front of the fire-box with about three feet to hold on to and included a 'dart' with wedge-shaped end for pushing under clinker-cake, a 'pricker' with right-angle end for raking the fire or for poking between fire-bars, and a 'spade' for lifting clinker or anything else out of the fire-box. Even near the end of steam in Britain, many of the largest locomotives were provided with fire-irons too weak to be of much use unless the fire was right down to dull red. Long fire-irons of reasonable strength were very heavy to handle. It is easy to understand, therefore, that on mounting the footplate to start a day's work, an engine-man's first concern was to make sure that there was enough water in the boiler and the second was to see what kind of coal they had got.

Over the years the work of firemen naturally become harder as the size and power of locomotives increased. In Great Britain, firing was not usually outrageously hard except perhaps on Garratt-type 4/2–6–6–2 locomotives used by the LMS for hauling heavy goods trains on the ex-Midland main line. In America, however, with much larger locomotives (hand-fired on grate areas up to 70 sq. ft.) firemen's work could be so very hard that it was formally laid down in 1938 that any engine with grate-area exceeding 50 sq. ft. had to have a 'mechanical stoker'. In the finally accepted form of that device on locomotives, small coal (about two inches cube) was moved by a screw-conveyor from the tender to the fire-hole whence it was blown by steam jets on to the coal already burning in the fire-box. That a fire-bed 100 sq. ft. in area could be kept covered to a uniform depth of a few inches by five steam jets under the fire-hole has always seemed to the writer to be a miracle comparable with that of the Giffard injector. Moreover the fire died down so quickly after the stoker was stopped that ashpan dampers were superfluous. With fire-bars rockable by the fireman so that clinker could be readily broken up, mechanical stokers could be worked hard enough to make steam with low-grade coal. The very nature of the steam-jet stoker gave every opportunity for the smaller pieces of coal to be carried up and through the tubes without burning, and so the stoker was very wasteful of coal at high combustion-rates. In most circumstances

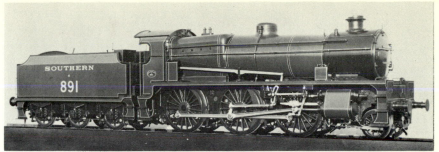

a. SR Class U1 3-cylinder 2–6–0 No. 891

b. Italian State Railways 2–6–0 No. 64004
with inside cylinders but outside valves

c. Southern Pacific 2/2–6–0 No. 502 with Vanderbilt tender

d. LNW Prince of Wales class 4–6–0 No. 2520

Plate 7

a. GW 2-cylinder 4–6–0 No. 2908 with down Birmingham express near Greenford

b. LSW 4-cylinder 4–6–0 No. 443 with down Cornwall express near Earlsfield

c. Up Manchester express behind poppet-valve Claughton LMS No. 5908 over-filling tender with water at Castlethorpe troughs

Plate 8

hand-firing that was not so heavy as to overtax the fireman was more economical than mechanical stoking which was tried several times in Britain but never won favour.

Although an oil-jet can easily be arranged to produce a nicely controlled flame, oil-firing of steam locomotives was not successfully accomplished without considerable experiment with fire-brick linings in fire-boxes. After sound procedures had been established, oil was naturally preferred as a fuel for steam locomotives working in areas adjoining oil-fields; there oil could be less expensive than coal but in most other regions it was not.

A great convenience of liquid fuel was ease of conveyance from storage tanks to locomotive tenders and thence to fire-boxes. It even made it practicable to place the tender at the smoke-box end of the locomotive and consequently to run with the cab leading at the fire-box end. Thus, the crew escaped smoke and hot gas from the chimney and this was very advantageous when working hard in a tunnel. On the other hand, engine-men used to working on single-line routes with 40 ft of boiler ahead of them felt very vulnerable indeed on a cab-in-front locomotive with only thin sheets of steel and glass to protect them when in collision with road vehicles or other trains. Nevertheless the Southern Pacific Rail Road adopted this construction in 1910 and were buying 4–8–8–2 arrangements of it as late as 1937.

Because a by-product of a process used for making gas for train-lighting was a tarry oil that was difficult to throw away without causing offence, the Great Eastern Railway used it as fuel for some years in a number of main line passenger locomotives. This gave such satisfaction that oil-burning was extended beyond the limit of the available waste oil. For a time the Great Eastern could buy oil good enough for burning in this way as a less expensive alternative to coal, but a rising demand for oil for other purposes soon changed the situation and oil-firing ended in Britain except during coal-strikes in 1912, 1921 and 1926. On these occasions a number of British railways converted a few standard locomotives to oil-firing as a supplementary action to the importation of coal.

Industrial difficulties in mining British coal after World War II led the government to assist railways in establishing oil-firing of steam locomotives, but after a good deal of equipment had been installed it was discovered that oil could no longer be bought at a price that would make it competitive with coal as a fuel in steam locomotives. By that time the diesel-engined railway locomotive was becoming established and, being able to get from oil about five times as much useful work as it would yield in a steam loco-motive, it was a far more appropriate consumer of imported oil.

EFFICIENCY

In general parlance, the word 'efficiency' has only a vague significance, but for any specific purpose in technology it is usually definable quite rigor-ously. For example, the overall efficiency of a steam locomotive as a 'heat engine' may be defined as the ratio of useful work it does in pulling its train to the heat energy in the coal that it consumes in doing so. The highest efficiency attained by a steam locomotive was about 7 per cent., which means that 93 per cent. of the heat energy in the fuel was dissipated to no useful purpose. This is so depressing that it was usual to express efficiency in some other way; what was common was to say that a locomotive con-sumed for instance, 2.8 lb. of coal per drawbar horse-power hour. From this one could deduce that it was more efficient than one that used 3.5 lb. of similar coal to the same end, without being conscious of the fact that both of them were extremely wasteful.

Such figures as the foregoing referred to a selected period during con-tinuous running. In actual service, the overall efficiency during a whole day of ordinary service might well be less than three per cent. because of the amount of coal required to get the boiler from cold up to working pressure in the first instance, the amount consumed during periods of standing idle and the amount remaining in the fire-box at the end of the last period of pay-load pulling. But ignoring this loss and concentrating on tests in actual running, it may be said that a good locomotive using superheated steam and working pretty hard in pulling a heavy train at 50 to 60 mph could get along on 3 to $3\frac{1}{2}$ lb. of coal per drawbar horsepower hour; this corresponds to an efficiency of about 6 per cent.

If the locomotive were worked much harder than this and produced steam faster by reason of higher fire-box temperature, the efficiency would fall by reason of extra loss in the hotter smoke-box gases and by the greater rate of loss in unburnt coal lifted off the fire by the stronger draught. In British practice it was unusual for a locomotive to develop more than about 35 drawbar horsepower per square foot of grate area for any period greater than about an hour. Up to twice that amount might be developed for a minute or two, but it would be accompanied by such a flow of unburned coal into the smoke-box and perhaps out of the chimney that the fireman would be convinced that the operation was much too wasteful to allow it to continue even if he could keep up with it. Not only was the coal being wastefully whipped off the fire, but if the effort was requiring late cut-off in the cylinders, steam was probably being used wastefully in them.

This latter loss could be avoided in designing a locomotive to be worked more intensively than usual by giving it appropriately large cylinders or, to express the point more generally, appropriately high nominal tractive effort, but what could be done about preventing intense draught from lifting small coal off the fire and throwing it away unburned? The answer is, 'Nothing', and the only easement of the difficulty is to avoid putting any small coal on the fire. If there is to be no excessive spark-loss from a fire under very strong draught, it must be fed with fuel in only large lumps that do not break up under the influence of heat but burn away each to a single piece that is by that time covered by later-fed large ones. It may be seen therefore that a steam locomotive that develops high power in relation to its size, and that is not at the same time wasteful in fuel, must be supplied with fuel of rather special physical characteristics. In his book that describes in great detail the record-breaking performances of his four-cylinder compound 4–8–0 locomotives on the Paris–Orleans Railway in the early 1930s, Ref. 16b Monsieur A. Chapelon refers to two fuels, Charbon A and Charbon B, but gives no details of them.

A contributor to the efficiency of these very remarkable locomotives was the use of a feed-water heater in which some of the exhaust steam is used to heat the feed-water taken from the tender. It was shown that in favourable circumstances a feed-water heater could save some 15 per cent. in fuel, but numerous trials of such devices in Britain failed to convince any railway that they were worthwhile in general service. Even the exhaust-steam injector, which is a simple kind of feed-water heater used by many British railways, had caused so much trouble by unreliability in the poor working conditions of World War II that it was specifically excluded from the standard designs of locomotives developed by the nationalised British Railways. This emphasises that strikingly good results obtained on special test may depend on control of a large number of details to an extent quite impractical in ordinary service, and so they may mislead the unwary.

Efficiency in using the heat in the fuel is obviously important, but fuel-cost was usually less than half the total running cost of the steam loco-motive. Its efficiency as an element of a railway system and not just as an item in a rigorously-controlled technical test for an hour or two is the ratio of the work it did in pulling trains during its life to its total cost in capital, running expenses, repairs and depreciation. As the former was never determinable with any semblance of precision, and as the latter was not much more reliably known, it has to be accepted that the whole-life efficiency (in this practical sense) of a locomotive in service could not normally be ascertained.

WATER

Everyone knows that the working fluid of a steam locomotive was produced by heating water so that it boiled, but had that been literally true, locomotive-men would have had much easier lives. It was impossible to obtain water alone in the quantities required for steam traction; what was fed into locomotive boilers was an aqueous mixture of dissolved and undissolved substances, nearly all of them detrimental in one way or another to the efficient operation of the boiler. In principle it was possible to analyse water obtained from each source of supply and to add to it appropriate chemicals in such quantities as to neutralise its impurities, but it was not practicable to achieve perfection in this respect. Indeed in the early history of the steam locomotive, no attempt was made to do it. It was soon found that any ordinary 'water' deposited solid matter in every boiler and if this was allowed to accumulate as sludge in water-spaces and as scale on the outside of fire-tubes and inner fire-box, there was overheating that could endanger the metal. So boilers had to be taken out of service periodically, cooled down, washed out, and cleared of scale as well as possible by use of scraper-rods pushed through holes unplugged for the purpose.

Even in such a small country as Great Britain, there was wide variety in supplies of water for locomotives. In some places the main impurity was acidic; in other places the water had the opposite chemical condition of alkalinity. The former corrodes metal; the latter deposits scale on it. It was accepted practice to give to a new boiler to be used in an 'acid' district a few preliminary weeks in an 'alkali' district so that the heating surfaces would receive a thin layer of scale that would protect them for a time against corrosion by their 'home' water.

Successive pick-ups of water from different sources could provide a locomotive with a mixture that was specially prone to 'priming' which is the production in the boiler of bubbles that burst less easily than usual. In consequence they fill what should be the 'steam space' in the boiler and water is then carried with the outgoing steam to the cylinders and the atmosphere. In this condition the engine runs at greatly reduced power, leaving a train of drops of dirty water, and is in danger of bursting its cylinder-covers by trapped water.

In spite of the difficulties and extra work produced by the use of bad waters, it was not until the twentieth century that any widespread effort was made to improve matters by applying appropriate chemical treatment to water supplied to locomotives. It then became usual to instal water-softening equipment where the available water was very hard, but the less objectionable varieties continued to be used as before.

An artifice that helped in keeping down the amount of sludge in the boiler was the 'continuous blow-down', an escape of water and sludge from the lowest point in the boiler on to the track. Engine-men did not like the continuous blow-down because they resented any unnecessary loss of steam or water from the boiler. To minimise the force of this complaint, an early arrangement was for the effluent to pass through a pipe coiled in the tender-water which therefore reclaimed some of the heat taken from the boiler by the effluent. Moreover, blow-down was continuous only while the boiler was being fed by an injector.

The LMS Railway adopted continuous blow-down on a considerable scale in 1939 with effluent discharged on to the middle of the track. This caused corrosion of vital parts of point-mechanism and so the discharge was moved to another position and then the right-hand rail became the main sufferer. This was a factor in reaching an eventual LMS decision to abandon continuous blow-down. More important was the realisation that unless continuous blow-down and the associated chemical treatment of water were applied with unfailing attention to detail the results might not justify the expense.

Chemical treatment ideally adjusted at all times to the current conditions in the water-supply required more exacting standards of supervision and discipline than had been normal in the staff concerned, and their imposition required absolute faith of the administration in the figures produced to establish the ultimate economic value of the operation. Perhaps its highest development was the *Traitement Integrale Armand* applied by L. Armand on the French National Railways. This meant adding to the water chemicals calculated to convert its impurities into sludge and to prohibit adherence of the sludge to the metal of the boiler. The treatment, which also included closely defined blow-down, had the substantial advantages of allowing the period between successive boiler washouts to be multiplied by about four, and boiler maintenance cost to be divided by ten. Comparable results were secured by the New York Central, the Illinois Central, the Union Pacific and the Chesapeake & Ohio Railroads in the USA.

Water normally ran into the tanks on locomotives or tenders through a long flexible leather pipe (or 'bag') attached to a pipe on a fixed column, or under a high-level tank, or on a swinging pipe or water-crane. The pipe needed to be of such diameter (of the order of 18 in.) as to pass about 1000 gallons of water per minute with the head normally available at the site. The lever or wheel for the control-valve was usually on the ground, whereas the bag had to be placed in the filling hole high on the tender and so two men were required for quick filling. Where water was taken at a station platform, regular train-watching enthusiasts were often glad to work the handle so that the driver need not leave the footplate. Such assistants knew enough to keep well back when, after the tank had been filled, and the water turned off, the fireman cast the bag off the tender.

More dramatic even than this was the British practice of picking up water by a moving tender from a trough between the rails. This was a British invention, widely used in Britain but surprisingly little in other countries. The idea was conceived in the Crewe Works of the LNWR, was tried out in the works and was applied in service in 1860 under the direction of John Ramsbottom, Locomotive Superintendent of the LNWR. The site, on the main Holyhead line near Llandudno Junction, was chosen to enable engines of the 'Irish Mail' to run non-stop from Chester to Holyhead even when heavy weather was using up a lot of coal and water. The troughs were moved some years later to a site near Abergele, a few miles to the west, because a more reliable supply of water was found there. The LNW was also distinctive in having water troughs on all four lines in the parallel Diggle Tunnels on the route between Manchester and Huddersfield. The LY route from Liverpool to Hull had six sets of troughs at an average spacing of only about 18 miles between Fazakerley and Whitley Bridge.

Water troughs required a level length of track approached in each direction by a drop of about 12 in., so that a scoop lowered by the fireman from the underside of the tender dipped still further into the water in the trough. Water caught by the scoop was guided upwards to a dome on the top of the tank and dropped thence into the tank. If the fireman had not lifted the scoop clear of the water when the tank was full, the succeeding flow of water lifted the lid on the filling hole, flooded the coal on the tender and spilled over the sides and back with general discomfort and possible danger for the occupants of the vehicle behind the tender. Picking up water 'on the fly' enabled long non-stop runs to be made with small tenders, it was convenient for the engine-men, it made a splendid spectacle for line-side watchers, but it was potentially dangerous to adjacent trains on which windows might be broken by overflow of water and displaced coal.

The maximum pick-up of water from any particular trough was usually achieved at a speed of about 35 mph and so where an engine required all the water it could get, speed would be reduced to that figure in passing over the trough. Otherwise there was no reluctance to pick up water at any speed, but the higher the speed the greater the loss of water in splash and the greater the risk of over-spilling. On the New York Central system, it was a rule that speed be reduced to not more than 55 mph when picking up water unless it was clear that there would be no train on either of the adjacent tracks. An exception was allowed in respect of tenders specially made so that overflow water was discharged close to rail-level.

A great many engine-men firmly believed (without evidence) that the amount of water that could be picked up on any particular occasion could be increased by running over the trough with the brakes applied to the wheels of the tender. The idea was that the drag on the brake blocks pulled the tender down against the resistance of the springs so that the scoop dipped further into the water. There was something in this in respect of a tender with brake-blocks in front of the wheels but that was a rarity. Tenders in general had brakes behind the wheels and when applied they *lifted* the tender and *reduced* the dip of the scoop into the water. If the effect had been appreciable it might have dispelled the engine-men's mistaken belief, but only very careful testing could have provided any evidence on the subject.

LUBRICATION

With the twentieth century more than half spent, the subject of lubrication of machinery has reached such sophistication as to suggest that the pioneer locomotive engineers were lucky, in the primitive state of the art of lubrication and the absence of mineral oils, to find any way of keeping a locomotive safely lubricated. They had to make do with animal fats and vegetable oils repeatedly re-applied to sliding surfaces. They were certainly lucky (and so the makers of reciprocating engines have been ever since) in that ordinary cast iron, such as was naturally used for making cylinders and pistons from the very earliest days is, because of its graphitic carbon, to some extent self-lubricating. Moreover, saturated steam (used throughout the nineteenth century) is always on the point of changing back into water, and thus deposits on the sliding surfaces in a cylinder a liquid film which, though not a very good lubricant, is better than nothing. Furthermore, tallow is soft enough to spread at the temperature of boiler-steam and at the temperature induced by friction at most other sliding surfaces.

Steam locomotives were always lubricated on the 'total loss system'. Lubricant was fed by one means or another to sliding surfaces and when it escaped from them it was beyond recovery mostly on the track sleepers and the ballast. On lines where outside-cylinder engines predominated, the ends of the sleepers were heavily oil-stained and on superelevated curves the inner ends showed this more strongly than the other ends. Impressed by the negligible oil-loss from motor-car engines, O. V. S. Bulleid enclosed the inside mechanism of the Pacific he introduced on the Southern Railway in 1941, but the difficulties in the way of achieving oil-tightness proved to be insuperable and oil consumption was actually greater than that of a conventional locomotive of the same size.

Oil was normally conveyed to bearing surfaces by a combination of syphoning and capillary action in worsted threads (called 'trimmings') adjusted to give a drip-feed at an appropriate rate. Alternatively oil might descend (or be thrown) from its reservoir through a worsted plug in a hole. A later refinement of this was to replace the plug by a pointed needle adjusted in a fine hole to give the desired feed-rate.

Oil was fed into steam pipes for lubrication of valves and cylinders by a 'hydrostatic' lubricator. This was a reservoir containing a vertical pipe over the open top of which oil overflowed and trickled down the inside of the pipe into the main steam flow. The pipe and part of the reservoir above the oil contained steam that condensed on the cold outer wall to form water that sank to the bottom of the oil and so displaced an equal volume of it into the pipe. In a refinement of this, steam direct from the boiler forced the displaced oil through a number of separate nozzles pointing upwards in water in glass tubes. Flow of oil was therefore visible in drops that slowly grew big enough to detach themselves from the nozzles and was adjustable by the engine driver. This was a 'sight feed' lubricator.

The elimination of condensation on valves and in cylinders by the use of superheated steam affected lubrication considerably, and it was common practice on superheater-fitted locomotives to use a 'mechanical lubricator' (a box-form oil reservoir containing a number of oil-pumps worked by a connection with some part of the engine's mechanism) to force oil through separate pipes to be injected into the steam-chests and cylinders at appropriate places. Some railways, notably the Great Western, used hydrostatic lubricators on superheated engines for many years, but the general tendency was always to mechanical lubricators.

Over a large part of the history of the steam locomotive, axle-boxes were liable to 'run hot', usually as the result of inadequate lubrication. A large factor in this was that a great many axle-boxes were badly designed in that they had oil-grooves in the curved surface that pressed down on the axle. Such grooves continued to be used for 50 years after it had been shown by Beauchamp Tower in a classic series of demonstrations made in 1885 that grooves in a load-carrying area were entirely disadvantageous and induced risk of overheating. Oil fed to the underside of the axle was carried by its rotation into the loaded region and there it worked best when there was no groove to interfere with it. On the Great Western Railway, this knowledge was applied from about the year 1903 but most other British railways were 30 years later in making use of it.

Axle-boxes in frames outside the wheels (as under most tenders) were readily accessible but others were not, and it was common to lead oil to them through pipes from trimmings in oil-boxes that could be easily reached; some indeed might be in the cab. But it was not always easy to find space for such pipes or to provide support for them; in some bad cases they were liable to be worn away by contact with wheels or to be broken by prolonged vibration. Deprived of its normal supply of an oil, an axle-box in a fast-running locomotive would overheat and the resulting smell of hot oil would usually warn the engine-man that some corrective action was required if excessive damage and possible danger were to be avoided.

A large steam locomotive might have as many as 60 oiling-points and so in preparing it for a day's work, an hour could easily be occupied in replenishing oil reservoirs, some of which could be very awkward to reach. In early practice this work was done by the driver as his first job after 'signing on' but when short working-hours became the rule, preparation might be done by other men. Total consumption of oil (in cylinders, valves, axle-boxes and other bearings) by an average locomotive amounted to about one pint per axle per 100 miles run.

In the early days of the steam locomotive, oils and grease were much used for lubrication. When mineral oils became readily available, they largely superseded other lubricants for most locomotive purposes, but in the twentieth century grease began to return to favour in America. For example, the big-end bearing of a connecting-rod might be designed to accommodate a block of grease that was fairly hard at normal temperature but would melt and feed the sliding surfaces when they had been warmed up by running.

Injected by means of a grease-gun into holes in convenient places, soft grease was more convenient than oil as a lubricant for pins in the mechanism. The method has the great merit that grease fed under pressure into the middle of a bearing moves outwards and pushes dirt away from the outer edges of the sliding surfaces. Lubrication by grease-gun is an unskilled operation that was used extensively on American locomotives. In taking a train over a distance of, say, 900 miles the engine would make a number of service stops at which coal and water would be placed in the tender, the fire-grate rocked and grease-guns applied by the ground staff attached to the site. All this was done quickly in a fixed routine that required no cogitation or judgement.

RUNNING-SHED WORK

In general, the steam locomotive demanded a great deal of daily manual work of a hard and not very pleasant kind to keep it running. On completion of a spell of duty it returned to its home shed in a rather tired state and needed to be revived before going out to work again. In the nineteenth century it was common for an engine to be run exclusively by a particular driver and fireman and so it had rest periods as long (or short) as theirs. In later years, with engine-men working a nominal eight-hour day, this practice had to cease and a main endeavour was to keep every locomotive in service for as many hours a day as possible. For this reason the first operation to a returning locomotive was to re-charge it with coal, water and sand so that in emergency it could go out again immediately even though its internal condition was far from ideal.

The next operation was normally to shovel char (dusty, gritty granules of half-burned coal) from the smoke-box. Opening the door had to be done very carefully as quite a lot of still hot char might drop out on to the front platform of the engine and on to the operator's feet. The very much larger quantity that did not drop out had to be lifted out by shovel and dumped on the ground alongside the track or into a pit between the rails or into an adjacent disposal-wagon. This was always dirty work, especially in windy weather, and where there was not much standing room between the front of the smoke-box and the front buffer-beam, it was very awkward and even dangerous work. The ashpan was emptied by a man who stood in a pit underneath the engine and used a long-handled rake to pull hot ash towards himself so that it would drop from the front edge of the pan into the pit. He could hardly hope to keep clear of the dust and sulphurous gas spread about by this operation.

Arrangements whereby ash and char could be allowed to drop directly into water in 'wet ash pits' had some limited use in the later days of steam in Britain, but for a century or more vast quantities (up to a ton per engine per day) of dusty refuse were handled by the most primitive methods. There was no technical difficulty in the way of mechanically handling char and ash, but for most of the career of steam on rails it was less expensive to get it done by hand.

Each engine normally returned to the shed with only a small amount of fire on the fire-bars and this could be left to die if the engine were to be out of service for some time. If, on the other hand, it was not going to be allowed to cool right down, the fire would be raked through to encourage fine ash to drop into the ashpan before it was emptied and some more coal shovelled into the fire-box to keep the fire alight.

If, however, a day's work with dirty coal had left much clinker on the fire bars, the fire-box would contain a lot of ash that would otherwise have dropped between them, and all this would have to be lifted out through the fire-hole unless the grate had a group of fire-bars that could be tilted downwards, leaving an opening through which ash might be pushed into the ashpan. Alternatively, if the engine was to be left to cool down, two or three adjacent fire-bars might be pulled up by use of a long fire-iron, to leave a gap for exit of ash. The fire-bars could not be replaced until the fire-box had been emptied and everything had cooled down sufficiently for someone to go into the box.

If the incoming driver's report suggested a need for special examination of the engine, this might affect its next move which was otherwise to place it in the shed (if there was room for it) to await its next job. If its turn had come to be cleaned, that would be done in the intervening period. Cleaning demanded wiping over with sponge cloths and paraffin, followed by such drying and polishing operations as the current practice demanded. Complete cleaning required about two man-hours per axle and it might be done one, two or three times per week for engines on goods, passenger or express passenger train work respectively.

The labour expended on cleaning engines was very considerable and the results regularly achieved before World War I can hardly be imagined by those whose observations go no further back than World War II. The gloss shown by photographs was not exaggerated nor was it limited to the big passenger-train engines. Every locomotive, down to the humblest shunter, was well cleaned in Victorian and Edwardian times and some posed pictures of shed-staff tend to suggest that a good deal of the dirt was transferred to the cleaners themselves. How soon a polish became blemished depended on the weather and the route, but the boiler could be badly splashed before the engine moved from the shed by dirty water thrown out of the chimney when the vacuum brake ejector was started, followed by still more when a mixture of steam and dirty water came out of the chimney while the engine covered the first hundred yards from rest. In the old days when all engines were kept clean, some men might leave the most vulnerable parts covered with cloth until the engine had run far enough to clear its cylinders of water.

Periodically, roughly about every 100 running hours, every engine was taken out of service for washing out its boiler. This involved time for allowing the boiler to cool down slowly, after which it was emptied of water and ten to twenty 'washout' plugs were removed to permit the insertion of nozzles from which strong jets of water played on such internal surfaces as were accessible by this means, with the object of removing sludge. Scale was harder to handle and endeavours were made to dislodge it by long sharp-ended rods used as scrapers. Further application of water jets would swill detached scale into the bottom of the boiler barrel and the bottom of the fire-box water spaces, whence much of it would escape through openings made for the purpose. Not all the scale came out until the boiler was taken apart for extensive repairs or for scrapping. It was then common to find in it large numbers of flat 'stones' each with multi-coloured laminations corresponding to periods of running with different kinds of water.

The operations of cooling, washing-out, restoring the washout plugs, filling up with water, lighting the fire and making some steam usually occupied the greater part of a day. The periods of cooling and re-heating could be appreciably shortened where plentiful supplies of hot water were specially provided for the washing-out operation. Washing-out was usually accompanied by tube-cleaning, which meant running a wire brush on a long rod through each of perhaps 200 tubes 20 feet long in order to scrape soot from them.

Coal for locomotives was brought to running sheds in four-wheel wagons that were usually the railway company's property, whereas most of the coal wagons that ran on British railways before 1940 belonged to the coal companies and prominently bore their names. Perhaps the commonest nineteenth-century method of conveying coal from wagons to engine-tenders was to use a coal-stage close to an engine line and rather higher than top of the highest tender and to run on to an appropriately elevated line on the opposite side of the stage, coal wagons whose side-doors, when opened, rested on the stage and permitted some of the coal to roll on to it. Coal from the wagons was shovelled into four-wheeled trucks which when full were pushed by hand to the other side of the stage and there tipped so that the coal slid down a chute on to a tender. The truck-load was a rough measure of the quantity of coal supplied to each tender. This manhandling of coal was a hard and dirty job, but only very slowly in the twentieth century was there any marked tendency to supersede it by mechanical handling, although Ramsbottom on the LNW had made some tentative moves in this direction in the 1860s.

The type of coaling plant that became common in Great Britain was a ferro-concrete hopper, of perhaps 1000 tons capacity, over an engine-track. It was fed by lifting a wagon to its top (some 70 ft above rail level) and there inverting it to empty its contents into the hopper. From the bottom of the hopper, coal was withdrawn horizontally in successive lots of half a ton and allowed to fall on to an appropriately positioned tender. Built-in water sprays were lavishly provided but a great deal of coal-dust escaped them. It is necessary to refer here to the unpleasant conditions imposed by the handling of coal, char and ash because the difficulty in later years of recruiting labour for it was a big element in the decision to allow the steam locomotive to be superseded by the diesel.

Most running sheds had staff and equipment for general maintenance of locomotives and for minor repairs. The quality of the equipment varied with its age, and repair work in British sheds was usually done in Victorian varieties of rather depressing conditions. As the steam locomotive remained for over a century in the basic Stephenson form, it did not need anything different in maintenance or repair from what had sufficed in the 1840s and, by and large, it did not get anything much better.

Some of the mechanism in many locomotives was quite difficult to reach even for daily maintenance, but when repairs were necessary they could require men to struggle with refractory nuts and bolts in most cramped and filthy situations. Work inside a smoke-box was always dirty. Work inside a fire-box was sometimes done with steam in the boiler when some co-operative member of the staff volunteered to help out by enduring great discomfort to do a quick repair that would enable the engine to take a train in emergency. On at least one occasion of this kind, fine sprays of water from leaking stay heads were in such positions that the man who went into the fire-box took in an umbrella for protection.

RUNNING-COST

The activating reason for any technical development, even one so dramatic as the production of the puffing, spark-throwing steam locomotive, is profit either by opening a new market or by providing a less expensive alternative to some existing form of activity. Before the steam locomotive appeared, the common tractive agent for land transport was the horse and it is said that a sharp rise in the cost of fodder in England was a strong stimulus to interest in the steam locomotive-engine in the early 1800s. Certain it is that only rigorously supported estimates of relative cost could convince the management of the Stockton & Darlington Railway that steam locomotives were worth trying. Even four years later, the directors of the Liverpool & Manchester Railway were unconvinced that the steam locomotive was technically reliable, but once that had been demonstrated by the *Rocket* and the full tide of enthusiasm for steam-worked railways had created a virtual monopoly in land transport, detailed costing seemed less important. Certainly the Victorian steam locomotive with expensive constructional forms, ornate decoration and meticulously maintained polish did not suggest that its owners had found any urgent need to cut costs to the bone.

Anyone who saw the tender of a large locomotive being loaded with coal for its day's work, or who travelled observantly for any considerable distance on a big engine working hard, might well form the impression that the main cost of running the engine was that of the coal it consumed. That was, in fact, the case but not so overwhelmingly as might naturally be supposed.

As every railway normally purchased coal for its engines there was no doubt about its initial cost. Expenditure on some other items was less easily evaluated, but broad averages could be established and some value might be derived from examining them. For example, proportional expenses representative of British and American steam-locomotive running in the twentieth century were about:

Coal, water, oil, etc. ..	40 per cent.
Repairs	30 per cent.
Wages, administration, depreciation, etc.	30 per cent.

While everyone could recognise that reduction of coal consumption was worthwhile, these figures show that there was a comparably large field for economy in repair work and a similar one in respect of numbers of staff.

Railway organisations in the nineteenth century were not brilliant in ascertaining useful statistics in respect of running cost per unit of transportation effected, but eventually the 'train-mile' came to be recognised as better than nothing, even though all train-miles were far from being equal. So far as the locomotive department was concerned, the 'engine-mile' might seem more significant than the train-mile. On British railways in the twentieth century, engine-miles were usually about 1.6 times as numerous as revenue-earning train-miles. 'Loaded train-miles' are commercially more important than total train-miles, and the ratio between them was as little as 1 to 2 where material, e.g. coal, was conveyed in wagons that returned empty from the delivery point to the loading point.

In the year 1921 for example, on eight of the leading British railways loaded train-miles per day averaged only about 30 per locomotive in the stock-list, although the London & South Western Railway, with relatively little goods traffic, showed nearly 50 miles. The average steam locomotive spent most of its time standing still.

To judge performance of any locomotive as a haulage agent, it is necessary to know how much mechanical work it did in pulling trains. This is determined not merely by train-miles, but by ton-miles and by running resistance per ton. As only a dynamometer-car can obtain the latter information, it had to be accepted that it was impracticable to ascertain how much useful work the average locomotive of any particular class had done per penny expended on it. A notable step was the initiation by Stamp of the LMS of 'individual costing' of locomotives with the object of obtaining factual information on the relative running-costs per mile of different classes of locomotive. Variation up to 40 per cent. was discovered and there was possibly even more on the unascertainable basis of unit of work done.

Steam locomotives that ran only a small mileage per day were extravagant in coal because of the quantity consumed in lighting up. This could be equal to that which sufficed to run the engine 50 miles in 'full flight'. On this account a locomotive that burned (say) 45 lb. of coal per mile over a day's mileage of 400 would show 60 per mile on 100 miles or 80 lb. per mile on 50 miles. This is mentioned to draw attention to just one circumstance that affected the relation between coal-consumption as measured during a load-test, and coal-consumption in service. Even in such a small country as Great Britain, the cost of coal placed on a tender was perceptibly affected by the distance over which it had to be brought from the mine. It could be very difficult to decide whether to buy good coal from a distant pit, or not-so-good coal from one nearby. The difference in cost of coal as placed on an engine-tender could be ascertained quite closely, and the less expensive variety would be used if average engine-men could get the necessary power from it. But even from one mine, coal could vary in quality from week to week and complaints about time lost by badly-steaming locomotives and differences in handling ash and in deterioration of fire-box and tubes could complicate the question as to whether it was worthwhile to place a contract for coal with Pit A or Pit B.

For a century or so, any British railway could obtain coal of quality up to the very best in the world if it was prepared to pay for it. After World War II had begun, that gradually ceased to be the case and locomotives had to be designed so that they could do their work with the inferior coals that were to be expected. This meant making engines bigger for any class of work than had previously sufficed, and – very belatedly – designing grates, ashpans and shed-equipment to handle more ash than of old. This was only following leads established elsewhere, notably in North America where labour costs had long been higher and fuel quality generally lower than in Britain.

REPAIRS

Protected against dirt and properly lubricated, sliding surfaces not excessively loaded need not suffer any perceptible wear in many years of service, but none of the sliding surfaces in a steam locomotive could be given such ideal working conditions. So there was wear at every sliding surface and eventually the associated imperfection in the operation of the mechanism became intolerable, and then some kind of repair had to be effected. Some things required repairs more frequently than others and it was common to take an engine out of service after, say, 20,000 miles of running for an inspection of the fast-wearing parts to be made at its 'home' running-shed, where there were facilities for regular minor repairs. After a number of such repairs there would be deterioration that could be corrected only by 'general repair' beyond the capacity of any running-shed, and the locomotive had to be sent to a fully-equipped works for dismantling. It was common for more than a month to elapse before the engine had been restored to something like its original mechanical condition for resumption of duties. Major and minor repairs used to keep the average locomotive unavailable for service for a high fraction of elapsed time and this was something to be investigated when competition was forcing railways to reduce running expenses.

Valuable reductions in repair costs were affected by setting up rigorous routines for establishing when any particular locomotive should be withdrawn from service for a major overhaul and by carrying out various repair-operations to a strict time schedule. The Crewe works of the LMS was the pioneer in this respect when it instituted the 'belt-system' of progressive repair in 1927, and even 20 years later the LMS was outstanding in its economical handling of locomotive repairs.

The distinction of the 'belt-system' was that every repair of every locomotive was carried out in a sequence of precisely defined operations. To each operation was allotted a particular place in the works and all were allowed a common length of time. Locomotives were moved from one operation to the next at predetermined times and that of the 'next move' was prominently posted for everyone to see. For such a cut-and-dried operation as the assembly of a motor-car the assembly-line principle was very well established, but it seemed optimistic to expect that similar precision could be achieved in simultaneously dismembering locomotives of different classes in different states of disrepair. In actual fact, by giving priority to the requirements of the pulling-apart-and-re-assembly line (the 'belt') and insisting that nothing be allowed to create any risk of delaying its next move, the time for which major repairs withdrew a locomotive from service was divided by about four, and the number of locomotives under repair at any one time was reduced to less than four per cent. of the total. The essential feature was that no locomotive awaited reclamation of its worn parts but was supplied with corresponding parts already reclaimed from another locomotive of the same class and properly placed for re-assembly without doubt or delay. After a locomotive had received a different boiler, a different frame and different cylinders it was perhaps difficult to say whether it existed at all, but this was only a rather academic point about which railway staff were less perturbed than were earnest amateurs.

Resistance to wear of sliding surfaces may be increased by better lubrication, by more successful protection against ingress of dirt and by use of harder materials. So it was often possible to reduce the average repair-cost of a class of locomotive by making detail changes that were not noticeable or even visible in any ordinary circumstances. Similarly a class of locomotive might be much more expensive to run than a superficially similar class of comparable major dimensions, but different in inconspicuous details. But the magnitude of the difference in operational cost could be ascertained only by the application of more rigorous costing methods than were usually practicable in railway workshops and widely scattered running-sheds. Because of inconstancy in the value of money, cost figures even for current conditions have only limited significance, but it may be worth mentioning that during the years 1927 to 1936 the total running-cost of the average LMS locomotive was about a shilling per mile; of this, repairs cost fourpence per mile and of this boiler-repairs cost as little as one half-penny per mile.

The table in Appendix II is derived from one included in a Centenary Lecture presented by P W Kiefer of the New York Central System to the Institution of Mechanical Engineers in June 1947. Individual costs are shown as fractions of the total cost; the corresponding figures for running of LMS engines in 1927-36 provide an interesting comparison.

The ratio of locomotive running-expenses to total traffic expenditure on British railways before 1940 was about 0.25. The eight figures for the four groups in 1938 and 1939 were all between 0.24 and 0.26.

5
STEAM IN SERVICE

THE steam locomotive, in general, required two men to run it and their vital duties were:

1 to make sure that the boiler water never got so low as to induce risk of explosion;

2 to make sure that the engine stopped at the right places and preferably at the right times.

These were safety requirements of prime importance. Operational requirements were more numerous. The engine could not keep going unless the fire was properly fed and this was the duty of the fireman. He normally made himself responsible for (1) although the other man, the driver, was officially responsible for everything. For this reason he had authority over the fireman but it was rarely necessary to apply it or, in the later years of steam, practicable to enforce it.

DRIVING

The name 'driver' probably derived from stage-coach practice where the man in charge of the horses had often to drive them mercilessly to comply with the time-table. The pioneer locomotives were so small and slow that no separate fireman was required. The driver might walk alongside his charge, just as if it were a carthorse and indeed might dally at the line-side for one purpose or another and then hasten to catch up to it. As locomotives became larger and faster, each had to have standing-room (a footplate) for two men and in due course the men were given some protection against the weather.

In the early years, when locomotive designers were gradually finding their way to constructions that gave reliable service in spite of increasing demands on locomotives, the driver at least had to be something of a mechanic to keep his engine working when things were going wrong, and he might devote some time to what were literally 'running repairs' without taking too much risk by not looking where he was going. This ceased to be the case as speeds of passenger trains rose, for then safety demanded an unbroken lookout at the track ahead. This was so even in Great Britain with every yard of running line rigorously fenced and every level-crossing gated and appropriately guarded. In countries where the railroad was not so completely protected, the driver's look-out duty was in principle much more onerous and especially so in darkness, in spite of even the most powerful head-lamps that could be provided. In Britain each locomotive carried one or more small head-lamps, set in such positions as to indicate not only the presence of a locomotive that might be moving, but also to describe the type of train behind it. The men on the locomotive could not (usually) detect from their normal positions on it whether any such lamp was showing a light or not. It was common to use oil-lamps, which could be extinguished by unfavourable conditions, and although signalmen could notice this, no train was normally stopped because it had no visible head-light. On the other hand, any signalman who saw a train pass without a visible red tail-lamp was required by rule to inform the adjacent signalman, who would stop the train for the fault to be rectified.

The engine driver's prime responsibility was the safe running of the train and so he had to see every signal that applied to it besides being on the constant look-out for emergency conditions not covered by normal operation of the fixed signals. In darkness he could do little more than see each signal-light at the earliest possible moment and the small oil-lamps on signals were remarkably effective even for the fastest trains in normal visibility. In fog, matters could be very different, and drivers had to rely on fog-signalmen stationed at each 'distant' (advance-warning) signal with a hand-lamp to duplicate its indication and a detonator on the rail to inform each driver that he was passing it.

Where the locomotive carried nothing to break the force of the relative wind on the driver, he developed appropriate facial hardihood reinforced in many cases by growth of an ample beard. Even after weather-boards, forward-facing 'spectacles', roofs and side-windows had become common, most drivers did a fair amount of leaning out of the cab to see earlier and more clearly what they needed to see and this, in conjunction with the draughts that were common in cabs, made enginemen's work a distinctly open-air pursuit in even the most protective type of cab. The fireman required, in addition to everything else, ability to remain standing on a floor subjected to constant vibration and a continuous series of unpredictable lateral movements. The intensity of the discomfort depended on the speed, the track and the imperfections in the mechanical condition of the locomotive; in bad cases, the fatigue on a long journey could badly slow down the fireman and consequently also the locomotive.

In the ordinary way the driver watched the 'road' and set the regulator, the cylinder cut-off or the brakes to keep the train 'on time'. The fireman fed the fire to maintain an appropriate steam pressure in the boiler and adjusted the injectors to maintain a safe water-level in it. He fought the coal-dust with water spray and he was apt to be burned by heat from the fire on one side and chilled by cold draughts on the other. On long runs he had the additional task of getting coal from the back of the tender to the front where he could reach it from his firing position. A badly-running tender could help because it could shake the coal down more profusely than usual. An engine might be run deliberately for some distance with hand-brake locking the tender-wheels so that they would be worn into 'flats' that in subsequent running would jiggle the coal down quite nicely. Such flats were more frequently produced unintentionally, when the engine and a lightly-loaded tender were braked heavily to hold back an unbraked goods train on a steep gradient.

It was not uncommon on a long hard run for the two enginemen to exchange jobs for a time during which the fireman might relax in the driver's seat (if the engine had one) and perhaps take some refreshment, while the driver did the firing. Drivers of express passenger trains were, however, not usually young men and while some of them might value a regular spell of firing as a means of helping to keep physically fit, others were sure that such exercise at their age would bring no ultimate benefit to anyone. Personal relations between driver and fireman were usually good but a driver who habitually drove engines harder than there was any need to do tended to be disliked by some firemen; they resented the extra work thus thrown on to them.

An awkward bone of contention was concerned with recovery of lost time. Some drivers were prepared to work a main-line engine hard with the object of bringing a late train to its terminus on time. In Britain the driver was not officially required to do this and so a fireman who did not believe it was an engine-man's job to recover time lost by other people might object to working harder than was required by a strict interpretation of his terms of reference. The driver could ease this situation by doing some of the firing, but not all drivers were willing (or even able) to help out in this way. When a praiseworthy recovery of time had been made, the driver usually got the credit, even though the fireman had done the necessary extra work.

Tradition played a part in matters of this kind; it varied from railway to railway and on any one of them it could vary between men from one running shed and men from another; it did of course vary from any one man to another. Some drivers would recover time where it was not difficult to do so; others would occupy the running time specified in the working time-table no matter how late or light the train. Still others would habitually lose time with always a ready excuse for having done so. In some countries, and France was a notable example, engine-men were offered bonus payments for recovery of time lost by others. Where a bonus was also offered for saving coal, engine-men might have to do a bit of meditation in order to decide whether it would pay to rush.

In North America, where drivers were called 'engineers', it was accepted that, in some circumstances at least, it was the engineer's *duty* to recover lost time by driving the engine as hard as he thought would produce the best result, and firemen had many distressing experiences on big hand-fired locomotives. With mechanical stoking, the fireman had little physical labour even though heavy working should double the rate of coal-consumption.

Reverting to ordinary hand-fired locomotives, it must be added that the commonest difficulties were not those associated with hard running, but those encountered in persuading the engine to do its normal job. Bad coal, delayed washout, unswept tubes, choked ashpan, for example, besides other unidentified defects, could cause an engine to fail to maintain its boiler pressure when handled in the ordinary way. Real experience, skill and initiative might then be required in working meticulously in ways not normally necessary in order to get the train over the road without undue loss of time. During most of the career of steam, there was not much trouble of this kind on the more important passenger trains because plenty of engines were kept in condition good enough to 'cover' them all, but during World War II maintenance standards deteriorated badly and never re-attained pre-war level to any wide extent. So a great deal of engine-men's work after 1939 was much more meritorious than a passenger might suspect from what he could see of the running of a train, but there was no way of assessing it numerically.

The commercially ideal railway is one on which the operating conditions are constant so that everything runs according to plan with no exceptions to demand departure from fixed procedure. This would suggest the possibility of running locomotives without human control and indeed with electric traction this is entirely practicable. The running conditions of a steam locomotive on the other hand never remained quite constant. Its 'steaming' deteriorated between successive washouts of its boiler; it might deteriorate in 200 miles by reason of sooting of tubes; it varied with the type of coal. The mechanical condition of the engine deteriorated between successive withdrawals from traffic for general repairs. Injectors could become temperamental. Imperfections could develop in the running mechanism, and in the hand-operated auxiliary mechanism. When an engine crew had its 'own' engine the men accommodated themselves to some of these defects as they gradually developed. Otherwise the men were presented with a new set of detail problems peculiar to the particular engine allotted to them, besides the general ones associated with fuel and water. The amount of intelligence and initiative applied to the job of getting the best out of an engine despite its defects distinguished 'good' men from ordinary men and provided them with some interest in what otherwise might tend to be a rather monotonous life.

This was something that the railway enthusiast and the amateur student of the locomotive found difficult to appreciate. The engine in charge of a fast express train was by far the most glamorous object on the railway system and as, in the ordinary way, no one was allowed to accompany engine-men at work, their life was naturally assumed to be glamorous and perhaps thrilling. It was in fact dirty, noisy, uncomfortable and also monotonous when it was not irritating. But even less glamorous than the work of engine-men when the engine was running was what they had to do before the engine left the shed and again before they left the shed to go home. Much of the work of shed staff was even less pleasant than the worst phases of that on the footplate.

FIRING

The fireman's job on every locomotive in every kind of service was to keep the boiler supplied with water and the fire fed with coal, coke, wood or oil. On a locomotive working at constant power, water and fuel should ideally be supplied at constant rates. In practice there might be considerable departures from this condition, but this did not necessarily imply any drastic fall-away from the ideal performance of the locomotive. It might be found impossible to adjust the water feed-rate closely to match the evaporation rate and it was then necessary to use an injector intermittently.

Where the steam demand varied, as on undulating routes or on trains that stopped at stations with short intervening distances, water-feed and firing were given corresponding variations. Where the power demanded of the locomotive was small compared with its capacity, the firebox might be so heavily charged with coal over a short interval of time that no further addition was needed for nearly an hour. Where the maximum sustained power was required from a locomotive, a fire of appropriate thickness (i.e. depth) was fed with shovelfuls of coal at equal (short) intervals of time and ideally the fire-door was closed between successive shovelfuls. This extra operation might be performed by the driver if the mechanism was conveniently arranged for such co-operation.

To get the very best out of any engine, it was necessary to maintain on the grate a fire-bed of nearly uniform thickness fed so that its surface was so far as possible incandescent. This could be done with care on most locomotives but was more difficult on large ones. Moreover it was rarely necessary, because in general the task set to a locomotive was within its capacity with the boiler in need of washing-out, with indifferent coal and with a not specially skilled fireman. So most engines could generally be fired without a great deal of care, and most firemen were able to get along without exercising any high degree of skill or attention to the job of placing the coal. This was especially the case on the largest British locomotives, Pacifics with 50 sq. ft grates which did much mileage with trains that could have been handled by engines half their size, and in earlier days would have been. So a big Pacific could have its fire built up in unhurried fashion before it was attached to its train in such a way that it could run 50 miles without needing any more coal to be added to the fire, and the firemen's job was easier than it would have been on a smaller engine. On the other hand, a big Pacific worked really hard could over-tax the physical abilities of the average fireman.

In less arduous circumstances the aim was to do the work on the minimum consumption of coal by adjusting the feed-rates so that there was no loss of steam by blowing-off at the safety valves and by taking back to the shed at the end of the shift the smallest amount of fire consistent with satisfactory running of the engine over the later stages of its last journey. It must be added that not every engine crew made any special effort about this; it was less bother to be less meticulous.

Firemen might be reprimanded for allowing the engine to produce excessive smoke. It was usually a result of adding a lot of coal to the fire and then closing the fire-door; in those circumstances it was usually avoidable by opening the door to an appropriate degree but as this reduced the draught on the fire, firemen were reluctant to do it during any period of demand for more steam. If closing the door after firing did *not* produce smoke it was a sign that excessive air was passing through a thin place in the fire, to the detriment of steam-production. In consequence, many engine-men had reason to believe the motto, 'No smoke, no steam'.

In principle there was, for every running condition, an ideal thickness of fire, but it was safer to exceed that thickness than to fall below it as any cessation of firing would improve matters in the first case, but could be very markedly detrimental in the other. So thick fires were normal and where adverse conditions were making it difficult for full boiler-pressure to be maintained, an improvement was usually secured by more careful feeding of a fire of more nearly ideal thickness. Obviously a fireman would not bother to do this in circumstances when it was unnecessary, and might therefore develop a reluctance to do it even when it could be advantageous.

The labour and awkwardness involved in placing coal on the fire were affected by the length and slope of the grate, the width of the grate, the size and position of the fire-hole and deflector plate, the distance between the fire-hole and shovelling plate, their relative heights and the proximity of objects such as brake handles and side tanks that limited the swing of the fireman's arms or might provide something for him to lean on. In many cases, firing required the fireman to stand with one foot on the fall-plate that covered the constantly varying gap between the foot-plate and the tender. In Great Britain, the Great Eastern Railway was outstanding in placing the fall-plate well back under the shovelling plate so that while firing the fireman could stand on one solid floor. On the other hand, one class of GE locomotive, the 4-6-0 (Ref. Z5) produced by S. D. Holden in 1911, measured about 8 ft from the fire-hole to the shovelling plate and this was awkwardly longer than the ideal, which is about 6 ft. A long high grate demanded a fast throw to 'land' coal to the front end of it. In this respect, the Drummond 4/4-6-os (Ref. 8b) on the London & South Western Railway were probably the worst in Britain.

Grates longer than about 7 ft were usually inclined to the rails at about 13 degrees; this drop towards the front end made it easier to throw coal there and moreover in conjunction with the vibration and oscillation of the engine caused the fire-bed to shuffle down towards the front so that there was less need to throw coal there; the fireman's main care was to maintain an adequate depth of fire at the back end, well within his reach.

Wide fire-boxes were not usually long and were therefore easier to fire than were narrow boxes, except that in shovelling coal into the back corners of the box the fireman's leading hand came close to the flames and needed some protection against the heat. This was usually obtained from a sponge-cloth wrapped round the hand and many firemen preferred this to the use of gloves such as others adopted in Britain after World War II. Where the back of the boiler was close to the front of the tender, firemen found need for protecting the backs of their legs from the heat when picking up coal. The Great Northern Atlantics (Ref. 4b) were offenders here, and their usually severe lateral oscillation was also a great nuisance except that it brought coal profusely from the tender down to the shovelling-plate; the fireman had only to get it through the fire-hole and the sway of the engine spread it over the fire. Firing could therefore be a not very arduous unskilled operation for anyone able to keep on his feet despite Atlantic antics and this suffices to explain engine-men's affection for those engines and their occasional development of very high sustained power when the crew were specially anxious to get home.

A locomotive fire at its hottest was blinding white, above steel-melting temperature, and although no furnace-man would think of looking into a steel-melting furnace except through blue glass, such precaution was most unusual on a locomotive. There were occasional murmurs from agitators that big fires were bad for firemen's eyes, but there seems to be no evidence that this was commonly the case. Where the top of the fire-bed was close to the level of the fire-hole the fireman could reduce emission of heat and light while he was firing by placing the first two or three shovelfuls of each 'round' immediately in front of the hole to form a black mass in the ingoing rush of cold air before the fresh coal was thoroughly on fire.

DRIVERS

After a driver had spent 20 years as a fireman on certain routes and had followed them with another ten years as driver of a wide variety of trains over those routes, he was apt to know them and the engines pretty well. Reflection on this makes it less surprising to learn that a good man could run a fast train in close compliance with the working time-table in complete darkness and without reference to any time-piece, pressure-gauge or cut-off indicator. He could do it with his eyes shut, relying on sound and 'feel' alone, if someone else observed the signals.

It must be added that there were men at the other end of the range of perception who became drivers of main-line express trains because promotion was by seniority, but never had any real confidence in themselves and were in fact a little afraid of big engines. Drivers' differences naturally showed up most strongly when conditions were abnormal. For example, failure to pick up water from a trough would convince one driver that he would have to stop specially to fill the tank, whereas another driver in the same circumstances might decide that the tank held enough water to reach the next trough. Worry about water was natural enough, but in some cases it was exaggerated.

Gauge-glasses showing the level of water in the boiler, although regularly replaced because the hot water corroded them, might burst without warning. A spare glass was normally carried and was substituted for a broken one, but a driver who found this to be impossible faced a difficult decision. Was it safe to go on using water without knowing how much the boiler contained? Officially the answer was 'No', but some dare-devils would keep going with both injectors in action till there were signs of water from the chimney and then stop the feed till the exhaust became dry again. No formal account of locomotive running ever mentioned such risky procedure, but it was only one of many that bold and confident drivers might use in an emergency.

When bad water conditions in a boiler caused it to 'prime', i.e. to send a lot of water out with the steam, some drivers would accept this as a reason for losing time or indeed for stopping for a change of locomotive. Others would minimise the effect by running with the boiler-water level right down at the lowest level visible in the gauge-glass and might thus get by with little loss of time.

Driver and fireman had of course to co-operate closely on matters of this sort, the driver taking the responsibility for irregular procedure and the fireman carrying out his instructions. There was always the danger that a driver's concern over 'internal' matters could cause him to miss a signal. It was for this reason that there was great value in any system that gave engine-men audible warning of approach to each 'distant' signal. In Great Britain, the Great Western Railway began to instal such a cab-signalling system some 40 years before the Harrow accident in 1952 stirred British Railways into corresponding action. The British Railways system was too expensive to be financially justifiable and even the Great Western system was dubious on that score. Something simpler would have satisfied the essential need which was to give audible warning of approach to each distant signal and to apply the brakes if the warning were ignored.

In British practice a man became a railway-engine driver only after many years (20 was not uncommon) of service in cleaning and firing. It is hard to imagine that many aspirants to foot-plate work liked the years of cleaning that necessarily preceded it, but at least until the end of World War II there was no great difficulty in recruiting young men to what had been recognised for a half-century to be a steady job. Rougher elements in the young had been quietened down by hard work and strict discipline before they were given a foot-plate job and engine-men as a whole were a respectable, reliable and conscientious body of men with a wide variety of off-the-job activities. Some undertook such long-term civic responsibilities as to be elected mayor of the town; another might win less publicity but more profit by running a modest brothel. Some engine-men could remain looking spick and span throughout a spell of duty in draughts and coal dust; others would look grubby and untidy at all times. The personal relations of the two men on one engine might be anywhere in a very wide range (fighting was not unknown), but what they did in running trains was rigorously defined by the Rule-Book and any proved deviation from it could be followed by some drastic penalty.

In most other countries the training of engine-drivers was broadly as in Britain, but there was a notable exception in France. There the eventual driver followed a course including study of the fundamentals of the steam engine and experience in making and repairing components of locomotives. In the early days of steam locomotives they might fail on the road in ways that could be corrected by an appropriately skilled driver but after a high standard of reliability had been achieved in standard locomotives the value of training drivers as mechanics may well have been questioned. In the later days of steam, repairs by engine-men were discouraged rather than otherwise and this suited some men very well; they were content to sit and wait for help to come regardless of delay to trains. Other men would do all they could, with or without official approval of their methods, to keep going when in trouble or to get going again after an enforced stop.

CABS AND CAB-FITTINGS

The designers of the earliest steam locomotives had enough to worry them without bothering about the engine-men who clung on to the engine wherever they could find a foothold. Higher running speeds made some specific 'footplate' essential and persuaded some British designers to provide weatherboards. Later on a weatherboard might be bent backwards at the top to form a rudimentary roof that might protect the engine-men a little from rain falling vertically in a dead calm on an engine at rest.

The severity of American winters led to the building of a cab on a locomotive as early as 1831 but the example was not extensively followed for ten years or so. In Britain, protection justifying the name of 'cab' was very

rare until T. W. Worsdell standardised one on the North Eastern Railway
from 1886. The Great Eastern followed in 1900, and other British railways reluctantly began to conform to the trend at intervals in the ensuing
30 years. Cabs could be too hot for comfort when standing in warm
weather but were much appreciated when there was a cold cross-wind.
Few cabs were anything like air-tight at the front and so, despite the hot
boiler, engine-men's feet could be frozen at speed in cold weather. Some
men alleviated matters by stuffing sacking or old newspapers into the
worst of the gaps. Diligent work of this character could be very beneficial
indeed, but it was apt to be undone by whoever had to get at wash-out
plugs near the bottom of the fire-box.

In the early days the tops of boilers and coal on tenders were commonly
not higher than about 9 ft above the rails and so a driver standing on a footplate about 4 ft above the rails could see forward or backward without
much difficulty. Later on, with bigger boilers and higher tenders, he had
to lean out of the cab to see backwards and often did so to see forwards
as the forward-looking windows might be quite narrow. Not every locomotive designer recognised that what was a satisfactory position for a
control-handle on a small locomotive might be unsatisfactory on a large
one. The brake-handle might be 4 ft from the side of the cab and this
was awkward for a driver who was backing an engine and had to lean out
to see the train that he was about to pick up.

An extraordinary example of indifference to operating convenience was to
be seen in the ninety 0–4–4 tank engines built for the Caledonian Railway
between 1899 and 1926. On these the tanks were built out well beyond
the width of the cab and they were so high that the front buffer-beam
could not be seen from inside the cab. So when the engine was being run
up to a vehicle or up to the buffer stops in a terminal station or elsewhere,
the driver had to stand outside the cab and peer alongside the tank while
his arm was stretched out to reach the brake-handle inside the cab. In very
few British locomotives was the brake-handle close to the cab-side where
it was always convenient for normal use and where it might be reached
even when in an emergency the engine-men had fled from the cab to escape
from flame, steam or boiling water. This did not often happen, but engine-
men were wise to remember that the boiler was always a potential danger
and that it was not easy for them to get away from it when the engine was
running fast in the forward direction. They might seek refuge on the coal
on the tender but the wind urged fire, steam and hot water in pursuit of
them in that direction and so it was usually safer to get ahead of the cab.

Trends in the second half of the twentieth century suggest that control of the railway locomotive (working, of course, on a closed circuit) may ultimately be effected by a push-button for 'Go' and another one for 'Stop' after prolonged consultation about the equitable sharing of the labour of pushing between the two men concerned. Even the earliest steam locomotives were not quite so simple as that because besides the 'regulator' that decided between 'stop' and 'go', there had to be a reversing lever to decide direction of motion and also a cock or cocks to control feed of water into the boiler. Appropriate use of the reversing gear could provide some braking action but the operation of stopping was a job for brakesmen on the train as much as for engine-men. In the course of time it became common to provide a cab for the engine-men, and concurrent development and refinement of the locomotive multiplied the number of auxiliaries to be adjusted until in the later days of steam the cab could contain an over-facing array of gauges, handles and hand-wheels.

Components to be controlled on the largest British steam locomotives included:

1 Regulator (of flow of steam from boiler to cylinders)
2 Reversing gear (set by a lever or by a hand-wheel)
3 Power-brake on engine
4 Hand-brake on tender or engine
5 Train-brakes
6 Two steam valves for injectors
7 Two water valves for injectors
8 Cock at top and bottom of each water gauge
9 Valve for steam for coach-heating
10 Sanding-gear
11 Ashpan dampers
12 Whistle
13 Cylinder-cocks
14 Blower
15 Water-scoop under the tender
16 Water-spray for damping coal-dust.

It was common for the vacuum-brake ejector to be inside the cab immediately in front of the driver's normal position and in some cases obstructing his view through the front look-out window. In fact a driver could see the signals that concerned him through less than ten sq. in. of glass because there was no need for him to see any one of them until he was within a few yards of it (and in fog this was all he could expect), but it was natural to want the earliest possible sight of signals, and leaning out of the cab could help in that respect. Some freezing conditions clouded the look-out glass so that leaning out was essential, and then eyelashes could be frozen solid.

For most of the period of steam on rails, engine-men in Britain were not provided with seats; even when such luxuries did first appear they were usually devised for use when the engine was standing rather than running. Later on, forward-facing seats with some upholstery became fairly common. Handles and hand-wheels on locomotives tended to be robust rather than elegant. At the best of times, strong hands were required to work some of them; at other times matters were less happy and designers had to remember that any handle might be assailed by a coal-hammer wielded by a big man in a bad temper. On any locomotive more than a few years old, the brass fittings usually had plenty of indentations where they had been hit by pieces of steel.

Reversing gear could be laborious to handle when the engine was shunting, and reversing levers might be uncontrollable when adjustment of cut-off was being attempted at speed. Power reverse or power-assisted reverse was used in a limited degree by some British railways but unless it was kept in very good order it could be more nuisance than it was worth. It was not used on the largest British standard locomotives, but it was essential on all the larger locomotives in America.

It was customary for the boiler water-gauge to be illustrated after dark by an oil-lamp mounted close to it so that the vital water-level could be ascertained at all times. Firelight reflected from the front of the tender provided adequate illumination for everything else after sunset. Direct fire-light illuminated the water gauge on the tender, which might be in the form of a shrouded glass tube or of a vertical steel tube with small equally-spaced holes which showed by the highest jet of water from them the water-level in the tender. Incredible though it may seem, some American locomotives, well into the twentieth century, had no such provision – the fireman had to climb over the coal and lower a long dip-stick into the tank to find out how much water it contained. Men who fell off at speed were usually killed.

On the Bulleid Pacifics of the Southern Railway and on a number of LNER locomotives built after World War II, electricity was used for headlamps, tail-lamps and cab-illumination. These experiments did not all persist because the extra equipment could be troublesome and was clearly not necessary.

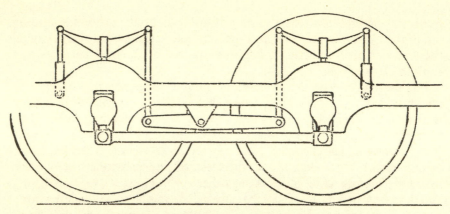

Fig. 17. *One side of a four-coupled locomotive with springs connected by a load-sharing beam proportioned to apply more weight to the left hand axle than to the other.*

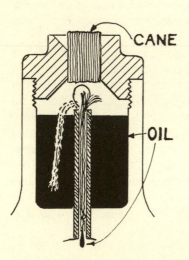

Fig. 18. *Typical oil box with 'trimming' of worsted threads adjusted to feed oil at an appropriate rate by capillary attraction. Porous cane prohibited air-lock.*

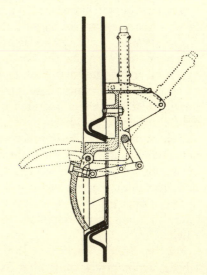

Fig. 19. *LNW type of fire door, opened by swinging inwards to a position where it acts as deflector plate*

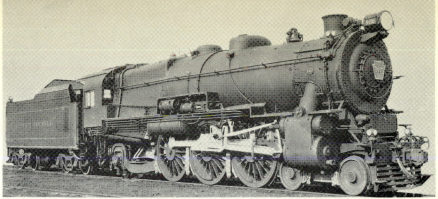

a. Pennsylvania K4s class Pacific No. 5494

b. GW No. 111, the first British Pacific to be built (1908)
   and the first to be scrapped (1924)

c. GN No. 1470, the second British Pacific. Built in 1922
   and rebuilt out of recognition in 1945

d. The first LMS streamlined Pacific, No. 6220, built 1937

Plate 9

a. One of the numerous LMS 2–6–4Ts of Stanier design

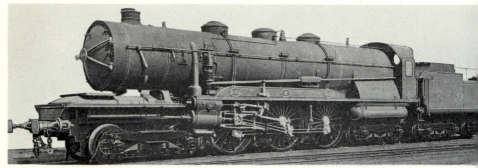

b. Nord (France) 4-cylinder compound 4–6–4 No. 3.1102

c. New York Central 'Hudson' 2-cylinder 4–6–4 No. 5405

d. LNE 4-cylinder compound 4–6–4 No. 10000 with water-tube boiler

Plate 10

Side-doors between engine and tender were valuable in greatly reducing the effect of cross-wind on the engine-men. It could waste coal by blowing it off the shovel, and this is a good indication of its severity. Nevertheless side-doors, although not uncommon in Scotland, were not normally fitted to British locomotives in general until the LMS locomotives built after 1926 began to raise the average. Engine-men's improvisations with sacking and the like were officially forbidden because of their disreputable appearance and could therefore be used only in darkness. On the other hand some railways did provide each tender with a 'storm-sheet' to be strung from the cab roof to the tender. Such a sheet provided useful protection against heavy rain, sleet, snow or cold wind especially when the engine was standing still or running tender-first, but it was usually too low for the fireman to be able to work properly underneath it.

Travelling tender-first at anything much above walking speed was so thoroughly unpleasant because of cold wind and coal dust or cold wind and cold rain that firemen would look where they were going only when necessary to see a signal, and drivers did not always overcome the temptation to do likewise. If the engine was holding back a goods train on a long descent, the fireman had nothing to do for a time and he might spend it, not on the footplate but at the other end of the engine in the lee of the warm smoke-box, affecting to be tightening its door when others might see.

The usual 'all-over' cab on tank engines was clearly much more protective than a storm-sheet when running bunker-first, but when running chimney-first, natural winds in some directions could direct on to the engine-men much stronger draughts than they might expect on a tender-engine with no special protection. Moreover when there was not much coal left in the bunker of a tank engine, backwards running could blow air through the coal and over the coal-shovelling plate and into the cab, enveloping the engine-men in a gale of fine grit. Another difficulty in those running conditions after dark was that illumination of the back plate of the cab by strong light from the open fire-hole could make it hard for the driver to see signal lights.

There was in Great Britain much substance for the common belief of engine-men that designers had either ill-will towards them or lacked experience and imagination about the manual work required to keep a locomotive going. It is certainly true that on some locomotives that brought world-wide fame to their owners and designers, engine-men had to struggle with atrociously inefficient details that did not affect anyone else. Mention of anything of this kind was rigorously excluded from the conventional officially-sponsored footplate story which on this account alone might be quite unrealistic.

THE DAY'S WORK

The day's work of an engine-man began by ascertaining from notices at the 'booking-on' point whether there were any special circumstances that he should take into account when running his train. Special speed restrictions were imposed where the track or an underline bridge was under repair; the normal water supply at a particular station might be cut off during some specified period. Although special restrictions were marked by appropriately placed line-side notices, engine-men normally learned about them before leaving the shed and might run harder than usual in order to offset the time to be lost by the delay.

A driver's first act on reaching his engine was to make sure that the boiler-water gauge was working properly; then he set about preparing the engine for its day's work. This included replenishment of oil reservoirs (perhaps 60 of them on a big engine) from supplies carried from the stores, besides examination of nuts, screws and locking devices that might have loosened on the engine's last trip. It involved checking that everything 'worked' properly in response to movements of the control handles.

The fireman's first act was also to check that the boiler-water gauge was working properly. He then livened the fire and fed it gradually so that the full boiler-pressure was attained just before the engine started its first loaded journey. He checked the supplies of coal, water and sand, the emptiness of ashpan and smoke-box and did all he could to make an air-tight fit of the door on the front of the smoke-box. Every locomotive was required to carry a set of lamps, detonators (for giving warning in emergency), besides spanners, firing tools, oil cans and so on. In the un-disciplined days after World War II a lot of time might have to be spent in obtaining replacements for missing articles. Although the fireman did his share of the physical work of preparation, the driver was responsible for its completion.

When the engine left the shed to pick up a long-distance train, the driver might feel that all his hard work for the day was done, whereas for the fireman it had hardly started; on the other hand, if running was to be over only short distances with a lot of shunting, the driver might have to work nearly as hard as the fireman. Such jobs however usually included a lot of standing time so that the effort required, when averaged over the shift, might not be great.

The easiest work for engine-men was to remain throughout their eight-hour day, or whatever it was, on an engine that stood in a siding at some intermediate station, in readiness to replace any that had developed a defect so bad that it was imprudent to run past any point where relief could be obtained. This was called 'standing pilot' because the engine might be attached in front of a main-line engine that was able to run but needed assistance. The word 'pilot' used in this connection was misleading, because it was not guidance or specially skilled steering that the train-engine required or received, but simply an extra pull. If the main-line engine could not be safely allowed to run any further with its train, the pilot would be substituted for it. A pilot engine might do no main-line work for months, although it could usually help with the shunting of vehicles within the limits of the station at which it was standing pilot. Its crew were paid in full whether it turned a wheel or not.

The most difficult job for a train-crew was the running of the average British goods train of loose-coupled vehicles over an undulating route. Such vehicles had no brakes that could be applied while they were running; the only usable brakes were on the engine, the tender and the brake-van. The men had to know the road intimately and to have a lot of experience to keep the train going at its booked average speed without breaking couplings. Such accidents not only meant loss of time but were also extremely dangerous as they might cause derailment that could obstruct an adjacent line carrying fast passenger trains. The rarity of collisions caused in this way is a tribute to the great care taken by trainmen in this most difficult class of work. To do it, the locomotive required strong and readily controllable brakes. To set against its disadvantages, the loose-coupled goods train had the advantage that, starting with all couplings slack, the engine could pick up the train of vehicles one at a time and therefore did not need to be able to exert any exceptionally high draw-bar pull. So British goods engines were not usually so large as the largest engines that worked heavy passenger-trains. The drivers of such trains usually found the job much easier than most of the others they had done in their earlier days on the footplate. For the fireman, the work could be very hard at times in the sheer shifting and shovelling of coal.

A class of service that could make quite hard and tedious work for engine-men was that of shunting goods vehicles as a full-time job. It was unusual in this sort of work to be kept on the go all the time, but it could happen. On the other hand, some 'turns' included long periods of doing nothing at all.

Every locomotive engaged in 'making up' or 'breaking down' trains in marshalling yards had its driver and fireman and also at least one 'shunter' who coupled and uncoupled vehicles. When the locomotive made a run of any considerable length the shunter might ride on it, but some railways avoided any need to do this by providing, with the locomotive, a four-wheel vehicle with long, low running-board and plenty of hand-holds on each side; it was much easier to mount this vehicle than to climb up on to the locomotive. In Great Britain, the Great Western called this vehicle a 'runner wagon'.

In North America every 'switching' (i.e. shunting) locomotive had instead of a cow-catcher a step, extending across its full width at about 15in. above the rails. This was for the ground-staff to ride on and it gave rise to a habit by such men of standing between the rails facing an advancing locomotive and mounting the step as it came to them. This practice was officially forbidden but it persisted despite periodic fatalities.

The driver's first duty after his engine had been coupled to a train was to make sure (with the co-operation of the guard) that its brakes were working properly. After that he had to be sure that the engine did not move till he had ascertained that it was safe for it to do so and had decided that it should. He would not do this until he had authority from the guard and permission from the signalman.

Although expected to observe the times quoted in the working time-table, British drivers were not officially required to carry a watch. Most of them did, but the others got on quite well simply by adjusting speed on the basis of long experience with some guidance from station clocks and from such others as they might see from the cab. It was the guard of the train who had to carry a watch because during each journey he had to record passing times at certain places and to give to the driver at the end of the journey a signed 'ticket' with a note of the time gained or lost.

When running, the driver had to observe the fixed signals and any temporary ones, and had to be prepared at all times to make a quick stop in any emergency. Consistently with this he was expected to 'keep time' in accordance with the current working time-table which included the passing times of the train at certain points between successive stopping places. He was required to do this without running at any unnecessarily high speed, and specific permissible maxima were quoted for particular points on the route. Exactly how he handled the engine in compliance with the official requirements was left entirely to him, although if he did anything exceptionally silly his fireman might have something to say.

The effort made by the engine at any moment depended on the width of the opening of the regulator valve, the point of cut-off in the cylinders, the boiler-pressure and the running speed. To start from rest it was usual to set the engine in 'full gear' (maximum valve-travel) and to open the regulator to the smallest amount that would suffice to move the train. As speed rose, the regulator was opened wider and the valve-travel reduced (to produce an earlier cut-off) in conformity with the driver's judgement as to what was appropriate for the running conditions. Some drivers believed that, once under way, the regulator should be opened to its limit and the cut-off adjusted to give the effort required. Others believed that it was disadvantageous to reduce the cut-off below some figure appropriate for the particular engine; they might use that cut-off and adjust the regulator opening to give the effort required. In general there was so little difference between the results produced by the two methods that the two schools of thought were equally justified. But each locomotive might have peculiarities of its own, and these could invalidate any generalisation. Cut-off indicators, in general, were quite unreliable and the average driver was wiser to rely on his own judgement (by 'feel' and exhaust-sound) of the effort being made by the engine than on anything shown by pointers and scales in the cab. Very few engine-men were deceived in that way but some of the less bright ones were apt to complain about an engine that did not pull as hard as they expected when they set the cut-off indicator to some figure that they thought was right.

Some drivers would make small alterations in cut-off in conformity with small changes in gradient. Others on the same job would run at fixed cut-off and fixed regulator opening and ignore the consequent variations in speed with gradient. Some would work only at cut-off figures that kept the reversing handle out of positions that they found uncomfortable when standing (or sitting) in their normal working positions. A feature of the steam locomotive was its adaptibility to a wide variety of running conditions, and well the engine-men knew it.

When a large locomotive was being worked hard the fire was a devouring monster, but in idle time between successive journeys it could be allowed to die down to domestic docility and provide heat for cooking. The shovel, polished by scraping under tons of coal and sterilised by hot water from the coal-watering hose, was nicely shaped for frying when held over a low fire. Any more than normally refined eater might bring with him a tin dish to contain the food while being cooked on the shovel. On some engines there were sites where potatoes might be placed for slow jacket-roasting during the last stages of the journey before lunch-time. Vessels in which water may be boiled are not conveniently shaped for carrying about and so enginemen commonly drank either cold tea or stewed tea during long spells on the footplate. Towards the end of steam on British rails, some engine-men's duties were such that some men could manage without bringing any food on to the job, but heat and exercise persuaded firemen that they should carry something to drink.

FOOTPLATE DANGERS

During the rapid multiplication of railways in the 1840s, when officials in charge of train-movements were gradually finding what unexpected things could happen, there were accidents that caused loss of life. So an inspectorate was formed and charged with the task of finding the relevant details and causes of accidents. Over the years the work done by the inspectorate in recommending changes in railway equipment and operating methods reduced the frequency of accidents to passengers on British trains to the extent that it was positively safer to be in such a train than almost anywhere else. As only a small proportion of railway employees were required or permitted to ride as passengers, the railways were not quite so safe for employees as they were for the general public travelling on them. There was, for example, more danger in riding on a steam locomotive than in the train it was leading, but even so, engine-men did not have an unusually dangerous job so long as they remembered what to do and what not to do.

For example, the regulator should not be closed while the engine is running, without first turning on the blower in order to draw air through the fire-tubes even when there is no exhaust steam. Without the blower, there is a risk of down-draught in the chimney and a blow-back of hot gas and flame out of the fire-hole into the cab if the fire-door is open, or less fiercely past its edges if it is apparently closed, because it never fits tightly. Whether or not a blow-back does occur depends on the height of the chimney, the relative wind, and the nearness of solid bodies to the chimney-top. When, for example, the engine ran fast into a closely-fitting single-line tunnel, a blow-back was almost certain unless the blower were strongly 'on'. Or, for another example, when an engine was running, smoke-box last, immediately in front of a wide vehicle higher than the chimney-top, there was high risk in closing the regulator unless the blower were working. What the driver had to remember was that if, when running, flame did come from the fire-hole the quickest way to stop it was to open the regulator (this was an important reason for having an easily-worked regulator). Blow-backs were not so numerous that drivers got much practice in reacting quickly to them, and some have died through leaping off the engine to escape flame from a bad blow-back instead of ending it by opening the regulator.

There is much greater danger in the breakage of an inside connecting-rod at speed, as the flailing end may puncture the fire-box or the boiler barrel and one or more fire-tubes, and then steam, water, hot gas and flame come to the fire-hole with boiler pressure behind them and if the fire-door is open the engine-men may be fatally injured before they know what is happening. Accidents of this kind were too rare to encourage a belief that no locomotive with inside cylinders should be allowed to run fast. Damage to a boiler or to a narrow fire-box by a broken *outside* connecting-rod was most unlikely, but a wide fire-box might be at risk.

Failure of a pipe-joint anywhere in the cab could produce a jet of steam that was dangerous to a degree depending on its position. The cause of one disastrous collision (Chapel-en-le-Frith, 9 February 1957) was the failure of a joint on a steam-pipe leading to the brake-cylinder on the engine of a mineral train that had just started on a long steep descent. The leakage made the steam brake ineffective and the escaping steam prevented the men from closing the regulator properly. The combination of the hand-brake on the tender and the hand-brake on the guard's van was not strong enough to stop the train from running away out of control.

It was common in Britain for each locomotive to have a running board that extended from the front of the engine to the back of the cab, and was wide enough for a man to pass forward along it to get ahead of any danger-ous commotion in the cab. In later years cabs were generally built right out to the limits of the loading gauge, and the only escape from many engines was on to the steps below the footplate level, but there was no safety there when the engine came to a station-platform. An admirable American provision for this type of situation was an emergency brake-handle on the front of the tender close to each exit from the cab.

Men on the footplate at the rear of a 100-ton steam locomotive 40 ft long, and immediately in front of a 60-ton tender, were not in an ideally safe place if the engine should run into anything at all solid, but they were in much less danger than are the crew at the leading end of a 100-ton diesel locomotive with nothing but a few layers of sheet steel and glass between them and the colliding object. Some men on steam locomotives did in fact survive severe collisions with virtually no ill-effect, but others were not so lucky.

6

UNCONVENTIONAL STEAM LOCOMOTIVES

COMPARED with practice in steam-power plants for stationary service or in marine service, the steam locomotive was primitive and remained so to the end. This was not for want of trial of alternative designs and methods of construction. At all times during the history of steam on rails someone was experimenting with something that was different and at least worth trying. But the net result of all such work on the ultimate form of the steam locomotive was negligible. For that reason it is impossible in a review of this sort to afford as much space for description of such special work

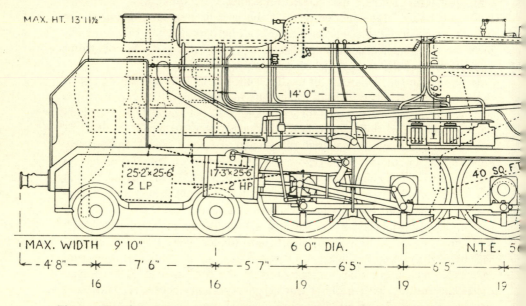

Fig. 20. Chapelon 4C/4-8-0 (16b) rebuild of Paris-Orleans Pacific. World record-holder for power in relation to size, and yet with high efficiency. Unconventional in having been designed to make efficient use of all the steam produced by working the boiler very hard.

as its technical interest could be held to justify, but it would be unfair to ignore it altogether.

The largest component of the conventional steam locomotive was the boiler. It was the one in which the conditions of pressure, temperature and chemical action were the most severe and it was the one that could be very dangerous if not handled with appropriate care and caution. It was the one whose internal condition required the locomotive to be taken out of service for a whole day in every six or seven. It was given expert examination at short intervals of time, as a safeguard against danger from unusually rapid deterioration. It habitually broke a number of its fire-box stays and so a close watch had to be kept on all of them. The Stephenson boiler did its job reliably enough at moderate working pressures but it was less happy at much above 200 lb per sq. in. and it was in some circumstances necessary to design locomotives to work in that range. In short, many engineers had the thought, perhaps not clearly defined, that something better than the Stephenson boiler ought to be found for the steam locomotive.

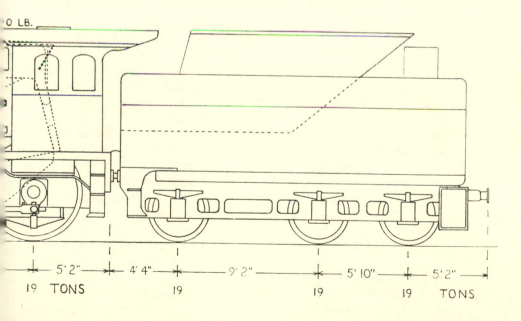

O LB.

5' 2"   4' 4"   9' 2"   5' 10"   5' 2"

19 TONS   19   19   19   TONS

WATER-TUBE BOILERS

In other spheres of operation of steam power, increasing use was made, after the start of the twentieth century, of the water-tube boiler and this seemed to be an obvious alternative to the Stephenson boiler in locomotives. For one thing, it had none of the stays that were continually breaking in Stephenson boilers. So water-tube boilers were repeatedly tried in locomotives but could not survive against their inherent disadvantages that

1 loss of heat through the walls of the furnace was excessive unless they were made so thick that little room was left for the fire-grate;
2 it was impracticable to keep the tubes reasonably free from scale deposited by such waters as could be supplied to locomotives in ordinary service.

An advantage of the water-tube boiler is that it may be made to work at much higher steam pressures than are practicable in the conventional locomotive boiler and it therefore offered the possibility of using compound expansion in circumstances that could permit it to show some useful advantage over single-expansion. This was never realised in regular practice.

The most famous water-tube boiler locomotive to run in Great Britain was the 'Hush-hush' 4C/4–6–4 No 10000 (Ref. 10d) produced by the LNE in 1929. It was designed and built in some approximation to secrecy and its appearance was startling in that the casing of the boiler extended to the full permissible height of the locomotive which had therefore no visible chimney, dome or safety-valve. The general bulk of the engine came as close to a streamline form as anything seen on any British railway up to that time.

The origin of the design seems to have been the idea that by using a boiler pressure of 450 lb. per sq. in. compounding could be applied with perceptible advantage in economy of coal, but there seems to have been no recognition of the fact that that result can be achieved only by working at a much higher expansion ratio than is practicable in the conventional locomotive. For the cylinders of No. 10000 offered not the slightest chance of this at any power output commensurate to the size of the locomotive. The pressure of 450 lb per sq. in. was far beyond the practicable limit for the conventional locomotive boiler and that is why the water-tube boiler was used. Its design was accomplished in conjunction with the Scottish marine-boiler manufacturers Yarrow & Co. It had the feature that the outer casing was a double wall and that the air fed to the ashpan reached

it by passing between the walls and was thus pre-heated by heat that
would otherwise have been wasted. The fire-box was provided with fire-
brick walls that were found to be inadequate and were thickened to the
extent that the grate-area was reduced to about 36 sq. ft, some 14 per cent.
less than that of the standard Gresley Pacific, so that unless compounding
and high boiler-pressure between them should produce some unaccount-
ably great advantage, this large locomotive would be less powerful than
those in common use on the LNER main-line trains.

No. 10000 did in fact rather uncertainly manage to maintain the leisurely
timing of the Flying Scotsman of the period on certain occasions, but
produced smoke in larger quantities than was customary in Great Britain.
The experiment of building No. 10000 was not a success and the engine
was rebuilt as an extended version of the standard Gresley three-cylinder
Pacific with a grate-area of 50 sq. ft in a boiler similar to those of the
Gresley 3/2-8-2s built for the Edinburgh–Aberdeen route in 1934.

MULTIPLE CYLINDERS AND FIRE-BRICK FIRE-BOX

On certain Sundays in the year 1908, observant railway travellers on the
Midland Railway between Derby and Leicester might have noticed a large
six-coupled locomotive with outside frame and fly-cranks, a Midland
chimney but no Midland red paint, evidently making trial trips. The
design, building and running of this engine had been effected in the
closest practicable secrecy and many years elapsed before even the most
meagre admissions were officially made about it.

It was designed by Cecil W. Paget, a Midland Railway operating staff
member who had studied mechanical engineering at Cambridge and who
had been impressed by the performance of Willans high-speed steam
engines driving electrical generators in the power house at Derby Works.
This led him to believe that it would be worthwhile to try, in a steam
locomotive, a combination of eight single-acting steam cylinders instead
of the conventional two double-acting cylinders. It does not seem ever to
have been explained what advantage Paget's cylinders might have offered
to offset the replacement of the simplicity of the conventional two-cylinder
locomotive by the complexity of the eight-cylinder layout and its associated
mechanism. Single-acting cylinders certainly avoid any need for crosshead
and slide bars and on that account each cylinder can be placed much
closer to the axle that it drives than is otherwise possible. This permitted
18-in. diameter cylinders to be mounted between outside frame plates in
positions that enabled four of them to be lined up with four crank-pins on

the middle axle of a 2–6–2 type locomotive. Two other cylinders were associated with cranks on the leading coupled axle and the remaining two applied driving effort to the trailing coupled axle. The layout was ingenious but it might have been hard to find room for eight sets of conventional valve-gear. At all events, Paget used rotary valves on a common central longitudinal axis with a shaft that was rotated by a geared connection with a jackshaft mounted under the footplate and connected to the coupling-rods.

The fire-box was built largely of fire-brick underneath a rearward prolongation of the upper part of the boiler. The 'fire-box heating surface' was therefore small and the water received most of its heat through the walls of the tubes in a short fat cylindrical boiler. The large grate (55 sq. ft) was high and would not have been easy to fire at high combustion rates, even though there were two fire-holes.

Partly because unrestrained bronze expands more with heat than does cast iron, the rotary valves of the Paget locomotive were liable to seizure and when this had occurred at high speed the extent of the resultant wreckage was discouraging. Moreover the locomotive remained immovable on a main line for some hours and this led to prohibition of further trial of it on any Midland running line. No further work was done on it and it remained hidden in Derby Works until it was scrapped in 1915.

The boiler had none of the stays that periodically break in conventional boilers, but neither had it the water-wall fire-box that contributes so much to the efficiency of such boilers. It is hard to see what advantage could have been derived from the multiple cylinders; they lacked the total enclosure of cranks and connecting rods that was a feature of the Willans stationary engines that had impressed Paget.

COMPLICATED GARRATT

Some 40 years after the trials of the Paget locomotive, O. V. S. Bulleid on the Southern Railway built a Garratt-style locomotive with a number of unconventional features. Each of these was well worth trying but the combination of so many of them in a single locomotive (even an experimental one) was asking for trouble and plenty was experienced. The conventional place for the men on a steam locomotive is immediately to the rear of the boiler, where the fireman is properly placed for doing his work and the driver is near to him. This proximity is desirable in the interests of safety even though it may place the driver 40 ft behind the leading end of the locomotive. This naturally imposes some restriction on his view of the landscape ahead of the engine, but it need not make much difference to his viewing of the signals that he must observe. Moreover the men do have some degree of protection in the rare event of collision of the engine with something ahead of it.

Bulleid was, however, a member of the staff of the Southern Railway, running large numbers of multiple-unit electric trains on each of which the driver is at the leading end of the leading coach with an unobstructed view through glass. Regarding this as something that might be claimed as an advantage of electric traction, and preferring not to offer a steam locomotive that should be different in this respect from what was common with electric traction, Bulleid provided his super-Garratt with a driving compartment at each end and a full-length corridor so that the fireman, normally working in the middle of the engine, should be able to reach the driver when special circumstances might demand close communication between the two men. So the boiler was set 'off-centre' and it and everything else on the engine were enclosed in a casing of maximum size and uniform cross section to give the aspect of an electric locomotive. The fireman's working-space was badly restricted and the atmospheric temperature in it was about 120°F, so hot that although one or two heroes accepted it for a few trial runs, no one could be expected to work regularly in it. Without the all-enclosing casing the fireman's quarters need not have been any hotter than in a conventional steam locomotive.

Each power-bogie had three axles, the middle one with three cranks driven by pistons in three double-acting inside cylinders fed with steam through sleeve valves. The valves had combined longitudinal movement and rotation and like Paget's rotary valves gave a great deal of trouble. Again one must ask what advantage the special valves were expected to have over conventional piston valves.

Driving connection between the axles in each power-bogie was affected by multiple-strand chains enclosed in steel casings. One chain connected the right-hand end of the middle axle to one of the outer axles and another chain connected the left end of the middle axle to the other of the outer axles. No one ever explained what advantage this complicated arrangement was expected to have over the simple, tested and proved coupling-rod readily available for examination and removal in the exceedingly rare event of any trouble.

A feature worth trying was horizontal location of each axle-box by a rubber mounting that permitted vertical movement by deformation of of the rubber and had no sliding surface corresponding to those of conventional hornblocks.

The boiler had no fire-box in the ordinary sense but it had two thermic syphons with nearly as many stays in them as an ordinary fire-box would have had. The fire was confined between firebrick walls that allowed far too much heat to escape and that were subsequently thickened on that account, with a marked consequent reduction in grate area.

The 'Leader' underwent a substantial amount of testing but its performance never equalled that of a conventional locomotive of the same weight and every one of its special features gave a great deal of trouble. This was not unusual with novelties, but there did not seem to be any prospect that even with everything going well the 'Leader' could ever justify its expensive departures from normality in design and construction. Three of these locomotives had been 'laid down' before British Railways took over, but only one was brought into running condition and its development was not deemed to be financially justifiable.

CONDENSERS

On the face of it, condensation of the exhaust-steam could reduce the back pressure on the pistons of a locomotive sufficiently to diminish coal consumption quite markedly. In practice that advantage is offset by the need for producing draught on the fire by means less convenient than the normal blast-pipe and chimney, and the weight and bulk of the condenser were so disadvantageous that the net gain was negligible.

A condenser could, however, be useful for other reasons, for example economy of water in regions where it was scarce. The outstanding example was the building by Henschel (Germany) of a class of large 4–8–4 locomotives for the 3ft 6in. gauge South African Railways. In these engines the normal blast-pipe was replaced by a fan driven by a geared steam turbine. A very large tender contained a nest of fan-cooled tubes in which the exhaust steam was condensed.

Some tank-engines could discharge their exhaust steam on to the surface of the cold water in their tanks and some could inject some of the exhaust into the water. This was done to reduce the volume of steam emitted when working on underground railways but it did little to rid the emission of dirt and sulphur dioxide from the fire. The reduction in back-pressure on the pistons by avoidance of the restrictions of a blast-pipe was very small and it was offset by the need to use boiler-steam in the blower to produce a useful draught on the fire. At certain stations on the Metropolitan Railway every engine had its tanks re-filled with cold water after the water heated by the exhaust steam when condensing had been rapidly discharged amid clouds of enveloping vapour.

STEAM TURBINES

After a dramatic demonstration near the end of the nineteenth century, the steam turbine began to replace the reciprocating steam engine in the propulsion of ships, and as reciprocating motion involves more complication than does rotary motion, it was natural to consider the application of turbines to steam locomotives. There is, however, a vital difference in operating conditions as a ship's propeller can be started from rest with very little effort indeed whereas a locomotive needs to be able to pull very hard when starting and this is something that a steam turbine can do (if at all) only by extravagant use of steam. So a steam turbine in a locomotive was handicapped from the start and indeed at every re-start. Extended trials of full-size turbine locomotives by the LMS in Britain and by the Pennsylvania Rail Road in America showed no perceptible advantage over contemporary conventional locomotives of comparable dimensions. The turbine could compete only on long non-stop runs on roads without steep gradients. It would have done better if it had exhausted into a condenser and so also would a reciprocating engine, but the condenser itself was an unbearable burden.

As a large steam-power station can turn into electrical form some five or six times as much energy from a pound of coal as the ordinary steam locomotive can get from it, it was perhaps natural to believe that a locomotive in the shape of a power station on wheels (a good many would be required) might justify trial. This was done more than once, and in 1947 the Chesapeake & Ohio Rail Road obtained from the Baldwin Locomotive Co. three such locomotives, each rated at 6000 hp. A 4500-hp locomotive on similar lines was placed in service on the Norfolk & Western Rail Road in 1954. These experiments were no more successful than earlier ones; the 'power station' locomotives were less reliable than the ordinary ones and only in special circumstances did they show any saving in fuel.

7
BRITISH—AMERICAN COMPARISON

BECAUSE the steam locomotive was born in Britain it is natural to base a book of this kind on British practice and it is impossible in any reasonable space to refer to different practices in all the other countries in which steam has been extensively used on rails. In order to give some idea of the extent of departures from British practices some notes are made below on some of the outstanding features of the use of steam on American railroads. Very broadly, steam traction in most other countries was effected in a compromise between British and American procedures, although many countries had their own distinctions in detail.

The United States of America form a very large country that was highly industrialised by the twentieth century, and a large proportion of railroad activity was in pulling big loads of boxcars over long distances. This required large locomotives but was easier to handle than goods traffic in Britain because the American trains were fully air-braked, whereas most British goods trains were in the form of loosely-coupled four-wheel wagons that were easy to start but hard to stop since they had no brakes that could be applied when they were moving. All American vehicles were connected by a combination of central buffer and automatic coupler, self-engaging on impact but having many inches of slack which, while helping a locomotive to start a big load, by that very virtue gave the passengers bad jerks. British passengers never had to suffer this nuisance because passenger vehicles are connected by screw-couplings (invented by Booth, the Stephenson company-secretary) usually adjusted pretty carefully to exert a small compressive effect on the side buffers.

Early American practice in locomotive-design was influenced by the need for engines to run on tracks that were, by current British standards, rather roughly laid, and for them to be maintainable in service by the very minimum of skilled labour. The first of these considerations caused American engines other than those engaged in shunting to be built with a leading bogie or a two-wheel truck, whereas in Britain most locomotives

a. LNW 0–8–0 No. 2550 built as a 3-cylinder compound to an 1893 design and rebuilt as a 2-cylinder simple

b. Chicago Belt Railway 2/0–8–0 switcher

c. GN 2-cylinder 2–8–0 No. 472 built in 1919

d. LNW 0–8–4T No. 380 absorbed into LMS stock during building (1922-23)

Plate 11

a. Baltimore & Ohio 2-8-2 No. 4317

b. Pere Marquette 2-8-4 No. 1222

c. Chicago, Milwaukee, St Paul & Pacific RR 4-8-4 No. 206

Plate 12

had no such provision. The second circumstance encouraged designing locomotives so that every working part was readily accessible for inspection and attention, and dismantling and reassembly were possible with minimum effort.

Available equipment could produce bar frames more readily than plate-frames and so the former were adopted and became a standard feature of American locomotives. Outside cylinders were preferred to inside cylinders because they avoided the expensive crank-axle and because they brought the piston rods, crossheads and connecting rods right out into the open, ready to the hand of anyone standing on the ground near to the engine.

In Britain it was common to provide a 'running board' that extended all round the engine at about four feet above the rail level. The part of any wheel that was higher than this was enclosed in a 'splasher'; for large wheels, splashers tended to be large boxes. In America, however, the running board was set above the largest wheels and a splasher was simply a strip a few inches wide, bent into a semicircle close to the flange of the wheel, and so readily overlooked that it is common in Britain to believe that American locomotives did not have splashers. Certainly the wheels were completely exposed whereas the engine-men were thoroughly enclosed in substantial cabs with plenty of windows and a backwardly extended roof. The absence of large vertical surfaces under the boiler made the sky-line view of an American locomotive very spidery in its lower parts, whereas sandboxes and headlamp were noticeable items in the upper works.

There was no British counterpart of the American cow-catcher, because in Britain cows were carefully kept off railway tracks and so there was little risk of an encounter between a locomotive and any large animal. In many parts of America such meetings were not uncommon and collisions with motor vehicles on the numerous level-crossings of roads became so frequent that cow-catchers were re-designed to meet metal as well as flesh, and certain items of equipment were specially protected against flying fragments. The coupler at the front of the engine was made to drop well below its normal working position when not in use because otherwise it tended to hold on to anything it happened to hit, whereas the main aim in cow-catcher design was to throw the offender's remains clear of the track.

A very odd feature of American practice was that the discharge of steam and water from cylinder-cocks was projected sideways from the engine instead of straight forward as in Britain. Every American locomotive was required by law to carry a bell and for it to be rung continuously so long as the engine was running on a track on any public road. Moreover it was obligatory for the locomotive's whistle to be blown in a specified succession of blasts on approaching every road-crossing.

Near the end of the nineteenth century there was a period when strikes in Britain prevented locomotive-builders from coping with a demand for more goods engines for a number of British railways. In consequence, American-built locomotives were bought for goods traffic normally handled by 0–6–0s. The American equivalent was the 2/2–6–0 because America's usual outside cylinders would have created excessive front overhang on a 0–6–0. These imports enabled British locomotive engineers and engine-men to see for themselves how differently were some things done in America from common practice in their own country. After the skimpy bar frame, perhaps the most striking feature of these 'foreigners' was the surmounting of each cylinder by a steam chest from which it was necessary only to remove the flat top-cover (after unscrewing a few nuts) to be able to see and touch the flat valve. To gain similar access to a valve between inside cylinders was a very much more laborious business. It was also obvious that the boiler, together with its self-contained cylindrical smokebox, could be lifted off the engine after the removal of about a dozen bolts. It is sad to record that none of these highly practical features was adopted in any designs subsequently evolved by the railway companies that bought and used the American Moguls. One might think that engine-men would have clamoured for general adoption of the American style of protective cab, but it seems that they preferred to be cold and wet on a British footplate rather than warm and dry in an American cab.

But after these American engines had been running for a few years on the Midland, Great Northern and Great Central Railways, and a few American-built tank engines had been set to work in South Wales, some of the distinctively American constructional features appeared in some new designs of locomotives placed in service by the Great Western Railway. They were moreover perpetuated in a unique set of standard designs that covered Great Western needs for 50 years and that were not equalled in general quality by any other British design for more than twenty. Oddly enough, these otherwise excellent Great Western engines incorporated one feature (lever-type reversing gear) of American practice that was thoroughly out of date on large locomotives long before the year 1900.

Increase in size of American locomotives soon made even screw-reversing gear too laborious for convenient operation, and power reverse gear became normal for the biggest engines. One may well suspect the existence of a secret international agreement that power-reversing gear should never be provided with any positive locking-device; in America, as in Britain, power-reversing gears had a perpetual and apparently incurable tendency to drop into 'full gear' so long as the engine was in motion. A gradual movement of that kind could be noticed by the driver who could then take corrective action without much trouble, but when the shift was abruptly right into full gear with the engine at full speed ('nose-diving' this was called in America) the outcome could be disconcerting.

By using heavier rails and closely-set sleepers it was possible to permit much heavier axle-loads in America than anywhere else in the world, but in spite of this, American demands for more powerful locomotives enforced adoption of the articulation principle in big engines far more extensively in North America than anywhere else. The early articulated locomotives were for hard pulling at low speeds and compound expansion of the steam was used as in the original Mallet articulated locomotives back in the late 1880s. Some development had to take place before it was found how to make an articulated locomotive safe at high speeds, and to enable it to attain them compound expansion had to be abandoned. This development culminated in the Union Pacific 4/4-8-8-4s (built in 1941-44) each weighing 345 tons and accompanied by a tender weighing 194 tons when fully loaded. These giant locomotives are mentioned here, not because they were numerous in relation to the entire locomotive stock of the United States, but because they exemplify the chief difference between American and British locomotives, and that was in size. The articulated locomotives were about three times as heavy as the biggest non-articulated British locomotives; the general run of American locomotives were about twice as heavy. Another significant distinction lay in the general use of mechanical stokers on the larger American engines; without such provision there would have been little object in building anything larger than a 4-6-2 or a 2-8-2 as were indeed the limiting sizes of non-articulated locomotives in Britain.

There was an interesting, but as it turned out abortive, development largely on the Pennsylvania Rail Road in the late 1940s and that was the building of what are sometimes called 'Duplex' locomotives. A big two-cylinder engine naturally exerted very big loads on its driving crank-pins and axle-boxes, and a means of alleviating difficulties arising from this was to use more than two cylinders. The three-cylinder engine had been tried in America but it was not regarded with great satisfaction probably because inside cylinders had never been favoured. So the artifice was tried of placing, on a rigid frame, four cylinders not abreast but spread down the engine so that two of them drove one group of coupled wheels and the other two drove another group of coupled wheels. On this basis were produced a number of non-articulated 4/4–4–4–4 locomotives, each in effect a 4–8–4 with 'divided drive' by relatively small cylinders. The Pennsylvania T1 class (14c), with 100 sq. ft of grate-area, were among the largest passenger train engines in North America and each was able to pull 1000 tons at 100 mph on the level, but they were troublesome in slipping and in other ways, and being introduced when maintenance standards were not high were not ultimately classifiable as successful in a land where diesel locomotives were working well.

The parallel Pennsylvania development on the freight side was a class of 4/4–4–6–4 locomotives. At 276 tons, they were the heaviest non-articulated locomotives ever. They were longer than the corresponding 4–10–4 and their long-term performance did not suggest any superiority over a conventional locomotive of that type. These unsuccessful departures from the elemental form of the American locomotive were a sad feature in the last phase of steam on the Pennsylvania Rail Road.

The main difference, beside that of size, between the ultimate American steam locomotive and its British counterpart was that the former had a cast-steel bed in place of the British plate-frame, but some detail differences are also interesting. For example, every British locomotive or its tender had a hand-brake that was safe and reliable for 'parking'. Such provision was not common in America and one might see a big 4–8–4 secured by placing two pieces of 2-inch wooden plank on a rail on each side of a wheel. More elegant was a short length of steel chain similarly draped on a rail.

American engine-men always moved well away from the side of the cab while passing any train on an adjacent track, so as to be clear of anything that might project from the other train, whereas it was not common to take such precautions in Britain. After the first hundred yards of his running with any train, the American engineer would move his brake handle to 'on' so that he could judge from the resultant retardation whether the brakes were working properly.

American passenger vehicles were about twice as heavy per seat as those in Britain. A reason for this was the realisation that a train wreck would produce fewer fatalities if the vehicles were so heavily built of steel as to be virtually uncrushable by collisions. Passenger-train speeds were not so high as in Britain until growing competition from road vehicles and aircraft from about 1930 led to some acceleration of the more important trains, and steam had to work hard in 4–6–4s and 4–8–4s to make an end-to-end average of a mile-a-minute over 960 miles between New York and Chicago. The regular passenger traffic between these cities was of the same general character as that between London and Glasgow, and the ratio (about $2\frac{1}{2}$) of the distances is about the usual American/British ratio in railway matters (it is said that an American millionaire railway enthusiast once built a private railway twice full size but no details are known about it).

Even on their longest journeys, trains other than British did not usually run so far as 200 miles between successive stops and this was why the Great Western's Paddington–Plymouth non-stop of 225.7 miles could remain a world's record for 20 years. In the later days of steam, an American locomotive might run a train for as far as 1000 miles, coal being added to the tender at several intermediate stopping places. The New York Central made special efforts with short 'turn-round' times of 4–8–4s at the ends of the Harmon–Chicago length of 930 miles to show that steam locomotives could equal the useful availablility of diesel locomotives, but this involved the employment of 'hot men' clad in asbestos to clear out the fire-box ends of the tubes without dropping the temperature of the water in the boiler much below its running level. With such heroic measures some astonishing monthly mileages were achieved by steam locomotives, but diesel locomotives could be run with little demand on human skill or endurance and in a time of constantly diminishing availability of those qualities were bound to win in the end. But neither form of traction could prevail against the aeroplane that could cover 960 miles in two hours instead of sixteen.

Many of the older American railway speed-record claims are found on examination to lack sufficient evidence to make them credible but there are later, well authenticated ones that line up with reasonable expectations of maximum power developable by the later large American locomotives. For example the running of a 1000-ton train on the level at a sustained speed of 100 mph is a worthy feat by a steam locomotive of any size and several types of American locomotive have been claimed to have done it.

8
SPEED BY STEAM

ALTHOUGH the steam locomotive was devised as a plodding work-horse that proved itself to all the world by doing what it was asked to do at Rainhill in a steady methodical manner at more than work-horse speed, it gave another impression of itself when George Stephenson drove at more than 30 mph on the *Rocket*, as indeed did Braithwaite on the *Novelty*. Even race-horse speed was evidently to be surpassed by the steam locomotive before very long, and while some thinkers quite properly discerned danger in this, others became interested and excited. Although the primary concern of any intending traveller by railway-train might have to be the magnitude of the fare, the length of time to be occupied on the journey was also a consideration. The possibility of making a long journey by train in hours instead of by road in days could transform the lives of regular travellers, and so for them the speed of trains was something more than an interesting academic abstraction. How long would it take to get from A to B by train? How many miles could a train cover in an hour?

In the first 20 years after Rainhill, railways extended in Britain at a rate that was barely credible and in some localities regular trains could on occasion run on the level at a mile a minute. When competitive routes had been established between any two important places, the railway companies concerned inevitably tried to attract passengers by announcing that the time-tabled travelling times were to be shortened, but were not anxious to quote miles per hour lest some unexpectedly high figure should alarm the more prudent types of passenger. There was need to avoid any suggestion that the fastest train between A and B was not quite so safe as the others. Eventually, however, after 50 years' use of railways had shown that they were safe rather than dangerous, competition was intensified into downright racing of railway trains between London and Aberdeen in the summer of 1895. Simultaneously at 8 pm trains left Euston and King's Cross to get quickly to Aberdeen over routes that were widely separated until they converged at Kinnaber, 38 miles short of

Aberdeen. They were time-tabled trains, usable by the public to the limit of their capacity dictated by the need not to overload the locomotives, and the frequently revised time-tables showed which route was, on paper, the faster on any particular night. Accepting the usual understanding that no train should leave any station before its advertised departure time, the race to Aberdeen was not from London but from the last advertised starting time of each competing train from any intermediate station. This difficulty could be avoided by quoting only arrival times at intermediate stations, thus implying that the train was run primarily for passengers from London but not from anywhere else. At all events the shortest times by the two routes were recorded on nights when the time-table was ignored and for the only period in British railway history, distances exceeding 500 miles were covered at end-to-end average speeds exceeding 60 mph. The fastest run from Euston was in 512 minutes over 540 miles (63.2 mph) and the fastest run from King's Cross was in 520 minutes for 524 miles (60.4 mph). The former run had three intermediate stops (Crewe, Carlisle and Perth) while the other had five (Grantham, York, Newcastle, Edinburgh and Dundee). The two extra stops on the East Coast route would hardly balance the 8-minute difference in overall time and so even if they could have been omitted, the West Coast route would have retained a slight advantage in that their stops averaged about half a minute shorter than those on the East Coast. The running times were identical at 504 minutes.

This at least is what is found after laboriously sifting the masses of figures and verbiage that have been published on this subject, without entirely allaying all doubts about the reliability of the various reports.

The engine used between Euston and Crewe was a Webb three-cylinder compound and therefore not the fastest of 'flyers'. A *Precedent* (2a) such as was used between Crewe and Carlisle could readily have reproduced its average of 67.2 mph on the easier road south of Crewe, would thereby have cut a substantial seven minutes from the journey time and thus raised the running average for the 540 miles from 64.2 to 65 mph. On the other route a mere change of driver could have removed quite a number of minutes from the time from the start to Grantham as the actual driver, a morose veteran, was, like the Webb compounds, no 'hot-shot'. A lively 'passed fireman' is the right type for racing, although none could be expected to surpass old Robinson on No. 790. There was some fairly reckless running at certain places north of Newcastle on the East Coast line, but the highest speed attained was probably between Penrith and

Carlisle on the other side of the country during the extraordinarily fast run of No. 790, the smallest of all the engines concerned. The maximum was probably over 90 mph but no one timed it and not everyone would have known how to do so in the dark.

The immediately subsequent run from Carlisle to Perth without the usual stop at Stirling was perhaps the most notable effort of the whole race. It involved a very carefully estimated risk as the water-capacity of the tender was barely sufficient for it and the driver had to make the decision on the approach to Stirling. Omission of the stop could save five minutes, but there follow 15 miles of climbing, six of them quite steep, and the engine had to be restrained for fear of running out of water. This did in fact happen, but the last 16 miles from Gleneagles to Perth start with 11 down which the train could run quite fast without steam. The remaining five miles include a sharp hump and the time occupied in covering them indicates that the driver had used very little steam on the final stretch because he simply had no water to make up for it.

This race was quite exceptional and nothing comparable in distance can be discovered in Britain railway records for at least 40 years afterwards, but a non-stop run at 70 mph from Glasgow to Euston (401½ miles) by an LMS Pacific in 1936 surpassed the best that was done in 1895. Soon after that race, the railway companies concerned got together and agreed to discontinue unbridled competition. A specific understanding was eventually reached that no daytime train should run from London to Edinburgh or to Glasgow in less than 8 hours and 15 minutes and this was maintained until 1932. 'Night sleepers' were not similarly restricted and some ran faster, but to little purpose as the earlier arrival at about 7 am. offered no advantage to most of the passengers.

For a period in the early years of the twentieth century, a Caledonian Railway train was booked to average rather more than a mile a minute over the favourably graded line between Forfar and Perth and from that time until the middle of World War I a North Eastern Railway train ran daily at 61.7 mph start to stop over the slightly favourable line from Darlington to York. That this was just a gesture is clear from the fact that the train then stood for 13 minutes at York before resuming its journey to Sheffield. Apart from these 'snippets' and some rather similar ones by a newspaper train on the Great Central, no British train was booked at over a mile a minute until in the autumn of 1923 the Great Western accelerated a train from Cheltenham to Paddington to run the slightly downhill 77.3 miles in from Swindon in 75 minutes at 61.3 mph.

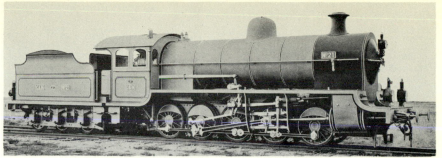

a. Servian State Railway No. 21. An elegant 2-cylinder compound 0–10–0

b. Belgian State Railway 4-cylinder 2–10–0 No. 4405.
Note curved weighshaft of reversing gear under boiler

c. Chicago, Burlington & Quincy RR 2–10–2 No. 6000

d. Midi (France) 2/0–10–0T No. 5002

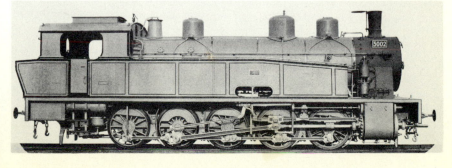

Plate 13

a. Great Northern Railway (USA) 4-cylinder compound 2–8–8–0 No. 2009

b. Erie 6-cylinder compound 2–8–8–8–2 No. 5014

c. Pennsylvania Class T1 4-cylinder rigid-frame 4–4–4–4 No. 5533

d. LNE 6-cylinder 2–8–0 + 0–8–2 Garratt locomotive No. 2395

Plate 14

a. Western Maryland 4–6–6–4 No. 1203

b. Virginian 2–6–6–6 No. 900

c. Baltimore & Ohio 2–8–8–4 No. 7602

Plate 15

a. Algerian 4–6–2 + 2–6–4

b. Chapelon 4C/4–8–0 rebuild of Paris-Orleans Pacific

c. Cab of LNW small boiler 0–8–0 (*see* 11a)   d. Cab of LMS *Coronation* class Pacific (*see* 9

Plate 16

In later years this train, which became known as the 'Cheltenham Flyer', was speeded up to a booked average of 71.3 mph.

The year 1932 was notable for numerous accelerations of important trains on most of the British main lines and mile-a-minute runs became not quite so rare. By 1938 there were in Britain some 80 daily runs at higher average speeds than this during the period of the summer time-tables; of these runs, four were at more than 70 mph. There were 105 additional daily runs at over 58 mph.

Exceptional running made in special circumstances include a non-stop trip from Paddington to Plymouth in 1903. The distance of 245.7 miles was covered at a start-to-stop average of 63 mph despite single-line sections and heavy gradients west of Exeter. In the following year a number of special trains ran from Plymouth to London in connection with the arrivals of certain mail-carrying steamers in Plymouth Sound. One of these trains averaged 62 mph from Plymouth to a stop at Pylle Hill, Bristol, and on the way reached a momentary maximum speed of about 100 mph on a sharp down-gradient near Wellington. Each of these performances was achieved by a double-frame 4–4–0 of the 'City' class (2c). The second of them was immediately followed by a run from Pylle Hill to Paddington at an average of 71.3 mph and a Dean double-frame 4–2–2 was responsible for this feat which remained as the British record start-to-stop speed till Great Western 4/4–6–0 No. 5006 added 10.4 mph to it in running from Swindon to Paddington on 6 June 1932. A less creditable and barely credible Great Western happening, not at all well authenticated, had been the running in 1906 of a newly-built 2/4–6–0 without a train at a top speed thought to be about 120 mph near Little Somerford, between Badminton and Swindon. Some 30 years elapsed before it could be certain that this speed had been exceeded by steam on Britain rail.

In 1906 the Great Western opened its shorter route from London to Plymouth by Westbury and the 10.30 am train began a long period of running the 225.7 miles without a stop. This was discontinued during a part of World War I but resumed later and remained a world's record for regular running until it was beaten in 1927 by the Euston–Carnforth non-stop run (236 miles) of the LMS 'Royal Scot' train.

The world record non-stop run by steam was established by a special train on the Pennsylvania Rail Road in 1876. A standard 4–4–0 with special provision for carrying extra coal and water ran the 438 miles from Jersey City to Pittsburgh without a stop as part of a piece of publicity (in the the form of a journey from New York to San Francisco, 3313 miles in

84 hours, nearly 40 mph) for an opera company. The Pennsylvania Rail Road also obtained some publicity for its part in this enterprise, especially because the same engine and train had run non-stop from Pittsburgh to Jersey City on the previous day. A British comment on this performance implied that it could be beaten whenever there might be any particular purpose in doing so. There must be many records that rest on the same insecure basis, but it does not invalidate them.

The closest British approach to the American record was made several times in 1948 when the Edinburgh–King's Cross *Flying Scotsman* was diverted from its regular route north of Tweedmouth Junction (near Berwick on Tweed) and its normal non-stop run of 393 miles was extended to 408 miles. Engines for the non-stop 'Scotsman' had special 'corridor tenders' to enable the engine-crew to be changed without stopping. Not everyone applauded this 'gimmickry' as it reduced tender coal-capacity to inadequacy for adverse running conditions and used engine-men's time extravagantly. So far as the passengers were concerned, the train might just as well have made a short stop away from all stations, for the crew to be changed. Had it been done at York, where speed has always to be reduced because of curvature, the loss of time would have been negligible.

A very noticeable landmark in British railway history was the introduction by the LNE in 1935 of streamlined trains booked to run at about 10 mph faster than the ordinary ones on the same routes, with a British record for steam of 71.9 mph from King's Cross to York by the '*Coronation*' during 1937–39. For pulling them a slightly modified version of the standard Gresley Pacific was developed and enclosed in a streamlined casing which probably reduced air resistance appreciably at speeds over 80 mph but certainly made it harder and less comfortable to gain access to many parts of the engine that needed daily attention at the shed. These trains occasionally reached 100 mph on down gradients, and it seems likely that they could, with a slightly abnormal effort by the engine, have attained that speed on the level.

War-time conditions from 1939 placed much extra goods traffic on British railways and locomotives became overtaxed, not by speed but by slogging along while in such bad conditions of disrepair and internal and external dirt that any useful effort from them seemed almost miraculous. Even after the war had ended, lack of good coal, shortages of material and labour, and general indiscipline made it impossible to approach pre-war standards for many years and never to more than a limited extent. The LNE streamlined trains, for example, were never revived although there was a slow approach towards their speed level by a small number of British trains after World War II.

The foregoing remarks about developments in the use of steam on rails in Britain refer mostly to outstanding running of the fastest passenger trains because readily available figures can afford some factual evidence on such matters. For most of the period of British railway history, however, the goods trains produced the bulk of the revenue and significant details of their running could never be readily ascertained by the public either by direct observation or through official channels. One might notice that the average British goods engine hardly increased in size in 70 years and that the average speed of the predominant loose-coupled goods trains was similarly static. After about 1923 there was a marked increase in the number of British 'fitted freight' trains of four-wheel vans fitted with vacuum brakes so that they could be run at average speeds of about 40 mph. Haulage of such trains was a job well suited to the so-called 'mixed traffic' locomotives, many of which had the 2–6–0 wheel arrangement, halfway between the 0–6–0 of the purely goods engine and the 4–6–0, the ultimately most numerous type of British express passenger engine. In time the 4–6–0 with coupled wheels of less than the 'express engine' diameter of about 80 in. became the accepted mixed-traffic type, and eventually it was realised that there was no real justification for any difference in wheel-diameter between mixed-traffic engines and express-passenger engines. The nineteenth-century belief that large wheels cannot pull hard and small wheels cannot run fast was never entirely extinguished in spite of 50 years' of experience that conflicted with it.

Tank engines, normally confined to short runs, were not usually required to attain high speeds and indeed many of them were unable to do so. But there were always some that could beat the magic mile-a-minute on the level and the LMS 2/2–6–4 tank engines (Ref. Z9) introduced in 1927 by Fowler were real 'flyers'. Running bunker first into Euston with outer suburban trains they would go through Willesden at over 80 mph like tenderless Pacifics, and on the ex-Midland main line one of them was timed at 90 mph. On the LMS, 2/2–6–4 tank engines became so numerous that many of them spent a good deal of their time pulling trains of less than their own weight on jobs that could have been equally well done by 0–4–2 tank engines of 1875 vintage.

The speed of British goods trains was evidently high enough for the railways to serve the community in a useful manner for 70 or 80 years and it is doubtful whether any practicable increase in it could have made that service appreciably more valuable to the customer. The cost of getting goods on to rails and getting them off again was comparable with the cost of the work done by steam in moving them between those operations. The main exceptions occurred where there was a continuous flow of heavy goods over particular paths and the outstanding example was transport of coal, the operation that caused the steam locomotive to be invented.

Outside Great Britain, goods vehicles on most railways had continuous brakes so that goods trains were 'fitted freights' that could be run in exactly the same way as passenger trains except that they were usually heavier and not so fast. There was a big contrast, for example, between long freight trains run for thousands of miles in fixed formation in North America and the short-distance loose-coupled goods trains that were common in Britain. For the former class of service steam locomotives were developed into larger sizes and types than those used for the most important passenger trains, whereas the opposite was the case in Great Britain. The main reason for the contrast is, of course, the difference in size of the countries. North America gave more scope for the economical use of steam to pull goods on rail but less for passenger trains when the aeroplane had become reliable enough for the average traveller.

STREAMLINING

When George Stephenson drove the *Rocket* at 30 mph at Rainhill as a kind of encore he must have felt considerable air-pressure, and later on he realised that when locomotives were developed to run really fast, the power expended in overcoming air resistance could be a large fraction of what was developed at the pistons. From that arose his suggestion that it might be valuable to shape the front of a locomotive in a way designed to mini-mise the air resistance at high running speeds. In other words, he visualised what later became called 'streamlining'.

It was not until the twentieth century was well advanced that loco-motives with streamlining appeared in regular service, and in Britain a little more time had to elapse before there was tangible recognition of the fact that if a locomotive and train are to be streamlined as thoroughly as possible, the rear of the train needs as much special shaping as does the front of the engine. In Britain it was the LNE that adopted streamlining in a determined way, but the GWR, having doubtless heard what was afoot at Doncaster in this respect, made a gesture that could be said to have given them priority in this development.

The Great Western contribution was limited to the modification of the exteriors of a Castle (Ref. Z6) and a King so as to diminish some of the discontinuities encountered by air in passing back over the surfaces of of component parts of the locomotive. The three separate splashers on each side were replaced by a long continuous one, sheet-metal fairings were placed behind chimney and dome, the smoke-box door was concealed by a near-hemisphere of about the same diameter, and the gap between the cab-roof and the tender was covered by an appropriately flexible material. It was probably not expected that these alterations would make any marked reduction in air resistance. They were undertaken without enthusiasm in the Locomotive Department in obedience to a directorial edict, and with expense very firmly restricted to a very small amount. The Great Western was the first British railway to apply streamlining to loco-motives and it was the first to abandon it.

Streamlining on the LNE appeared partly because it was a publicity feature of a special high-speed train and partly because, at high speed, streamlining might be expected to show worthwhile reduction in work done against air resistance. If the speed is high enough, it is bound to do so, but would it gain much at 80 mph? Wind-tunnel tests made by the National Physical Laboratory on LNE models indicated that a saving of 97 horsepower at 80 mph and 138 horsepower at 90 mph, might be expected from the adopted shape. That of the front of the locomotive was basically a horizontal wedge so that the tendency was to shovel up the air and let it pass overhead, rather than to elbow it out sideways, and behind the nose that hid the front of the smoke-box a smooth, gently curved steel casing led back to the cab. A rubber sheet connected the rear of the cab-roof to the equally high front of the tender. This sheet made things pretty hot for the engine-men except when running fast, and the main casing extending right down to the normal position of the running board trapped heat and fumes in a manner fairly distressing to anyone who had to inspect the mechanism between the frames, because it was too dark to see much without artificial lighting which for that kind of job normally came from a smoky flame from oil burning at the top end of a large wick. The stream-lined nose could be opened in the manner of a crocodile's mouth to expose the smoke-box door for the daily operation of removal of char.

In progressing from the standard LNE Pacific of Class A3 to its stream-lined A4 successor (Ref. Z8) the cylinder-size was reduced to make room for a larger valve in the cramped position alongside the inside cylinder. This made the engine 'faster' but in order to obtain the high nominal tractive effort appropriate for the work that the locomotive would be required to do on heavy passenger trains at the usual LNE speed, the boiler-pressure had to be raised and this demanded a stronger (and therefore heavier) boiler, although there was no change in major dimensions. The new boiler was about $1\frac{1}{2}$ tons heavier than that of the A3 locomotive and the streamline casing might weigh three or three-and-a-half tons, but the published difference in total weight was over six tons. (An American locomotive engineer once remarked that if he had been allowed to use the extra weight of streamlining to make the boiler bigger, he could in that way get more power out of the engine at all ordinary speeds.)

In September 1935, the *Silver Jubilee* streamlined train on the LNE between King's Cross and Newcastle started some four years of successful service after an unnerving demonstration that demolished some British railway speed records with many miles at over 100 mph, but it was never ascertained to what extent streamlining had contributed to this display. The 220-ton train was a plaything for the 103-ton Pacific under the streamline casing. It could climb most of the gradients on the LNE main line at 75 mph and so start-to-stop average speeds of that order were not infrequently achieved between London and Darlington. It was shown that the booked average of 70 mph was well within the capacity of the non-streamlined A3 Pacifics that occasionally deputised for A4s. It was never specifically ascertained whether the National Physical Laboratory estimates of power-saving by streamlining were realised in practice (this would have been quite difficult to do) but someone must have been satisfied, as some 35 streamlined locomotives of substantially unchanged design were eventually built by the LNE and retained their streamlining (apart from removal of two long shallow sheets that hid the valve-gear) until they were withdrawn from service.

On one special occasion, one of the streamlined A4 Pacifics with a double chimney, a special train, an imperturbably self-confident driver and a 19-mile stretch of downhill, reached a top speed of 126 mph. This is not known to have been exceeded by steam on rails, but is believed to have been equalled by a German 4-6-4 specially designed and built for high speed. A speed of over two miles per minute was so far above normal railway requirements and experience that no ordinary locomotive could be expected to survive it for very long, but the damage suffered by the LNE record breaker (No. 4468 *Mallard*) was slight and easily corrected.

As a counterblast to the LNE streamlined trains, the LMS introduced a corresponding train on the Euston–Glasgow route in 1937 and built more than 20 large Pacifics with streamline casings, but these were eventually removed and the engines ran the greater parts of their lives without them.

The story of locomotive streamlining in Britain was pretty well repeated everywhere else it was tried. It could have been worthwhile at average speeds round 100 mph, and it was a feature of all of the few British loco-motives known to have exceeded 110 mph, but at the usual running average of less than 80 mph its overall value was dubious. 'Internal stream-lining' of locomotives was an imaginative enthusiast's invention about which no detail was ever described. It was implied to be very valuable but it was never either defined or numerically assessed, and no one who saw the encrusted walls of 6-months old steam-passages would associate them with anything so refined as streamlining.

CONCLUSION

Power to move things was first obtained by man from the natural sources of wind and water through devices that did not demand refinement in mechanical construction; refinement could help, but it was not essential.

Power was first obtained from steam through slowly-moving mechanism that had to include a piston fitting closely into a cylinder. Some refinement in construction was necessary to achieve a useful result and further refine-ment could raise the efficiency of the engine very considerably. Steam was used because it could easily be condensed to produce sub-atmospheric pressure. The whole assembly was bulky because it included a boiler with a fire, a cylinder or cylinders, mechanism to derive forceful movement from pressure of steam, and a condenser.

Burning of fuel in an enclosed volume of gas and use of its consequent quick rise in pressure to push a piston was a much more direct way of getting mechanical power from heat, but the details demanded more highly refined technology and mechanism than sufficed for steam. When the necessary advances had been made, and the fast-running internal combustion engine became reliable, it showed great advantages over steam for traction on either road or rail. By the time it had vanquished steam on rail, many of the functions of rail-transport could be more conveniently carried out on the road. So a great deal of rail had vanished before steam vanished from what was left.

Baker Valve-gear

The general principle underlying the distinctive feature of the Baker valve·gear may be gathered from Fig. 21(a) in which L is a link that swings about an axis represented by A while its lower end P moves over an arc 12 because it is connected by a rod M to a crank-pin C moving round a circle with centre D.

If as in Fig. 21(b) the pivot point of L is moved to another position A_F at the same distance from B as is A, the path of the lower end of L becomes the arc 34.

The lower end P of the link L may therefore have any of the circular paths of radius equal to the length of L that contain the point B and lie within the range from 34 to 56.

Fig. 21(d) shows the path 34 of the pin P but none of the mechanism that defines it. A bell-crank lever is pivoted at K and in its mean position, one arm is horizontal and the pin at its right-hand end coincides with A. That pin is connected to pin P by a link N of the same length as the link L. When P is at the common point B of all its possible paths, the link N and link L coincide. (In the actual mechanism the links must therefore be laterally offset from one another.)

If P follows the path 12, which is a circular arc with centre at A, the bell-crank lever does not move. If P follows any other of its possible paths, the lever reciprocates in unison with P, but over a distance that depends on the identity of the path and therefore on the position of the upper pivoting point of the link L.

Fig. 21(d) shows the extreme positions of the bell-crank lever when the pivot is at A_F. From this it will be seen that at all times motion of the point Q at the end of the lower arm of the ball-crank lever is in the same horizontal direction as that of P. If, on the other hand, the upper pivot of L is at A_B, then the path of P is 56 and the horizontal motion of Q is at all times in the opposite direction to that of P. (Q is linked to a 'combination lever' as used in Walschaerts valve-gear).

Thus the relation between the movements of Q and P is defined by the positon of the pivot point of L, just as in Walschaerts valve-gear, the relation between the motion of the radius-rod and that of the lower end of the slotted link is determined by the position of the die-block in the slotted link.

The actual Baker valve-gear is not quite so simple as Fig. 21 may suggest but the essential kinematic feature is the same in both. A great advantage of the Baker gear was that its only sliding surfaces (those of the pins and the bushes in which they worked) were not exposed to dirt; any that did penetrate was expelled by grease-gun lubrication. In later practice, the bushes were replaced by needle-roller bearings and there was no sliding anywhere in the whole mechanism which was in that respect superior to all others. A disadvantage of the Baker gear was that as some of its links 'overlapped' and were duplicated to avoid offset loading, its maximum width was greater than that of the corresponding Walschaerts gear and this may explain why it was never tried on any standard-gauge locomotive in Britain. It was adopted as standard by the New York Central Railroad and used extensively elsewhere in the USA but not to the exclusion of Walschaerts gear.

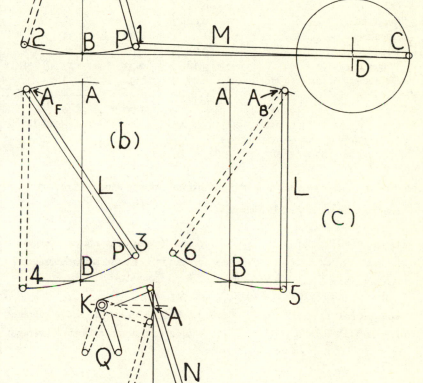

Fig. 21. *Diagrams to demonstrate the basic geometrical principle of the Baker valvegear*

Relative Annual Operating Costs

	New York Central 2/4–8–4 in 1946		LMS Average* in 1927-36
		Totals	
Fuel	0.34 ⎞		
Water	0.025 ⎟	0.38	0.40
Oil	0.01 ⎬		
Sand, etc.	0.005 ⎠		
Repairs		0.29	0.33
Shed expenses	0.08 ⎞		
Wages	0.18 ⎬	0.33	0.27
Depreciation, interest, etc. ..	0.07 ⎠		
		1.00	1.00

* For many classes of locomotives.

Locomotive running expenses as a fraction of total railway expenditure:

Average for six largest British railways during 1906	0.277	
Highest (NER)	0.290	(5 per cent. above average)
Lowest (GER)	0.250	(10 per cent. below average)
Average for the four British railway groups during 1937 and 1938 ..	0.2514	
Highest (SR in 1938)	0.2586	(2.8 per cent. above average)
Lowest (GWR in 1937)	0.2462	(2.1 per cent. below average)

TABLE 1

Some dimensions of locomotives

Ref.	Rail-way	Wheel arr'g't	Grate Area (sq-ft)	Weight (tons.) Adh.	Tot.	Wheel dia-meter (in.)	Nominal Tractive Effort (1000 lb.)	Date of first	Class or Builder
1a	GC	422	21	18	50	93	15	1900	I3
b	LNW	040ST	6	23	23	49	8	1863	(LNW)
c	GW	044R	11.5	27	43	43	8	1903	(Kerr Stuart) Rail-motor
d	GN	044R	9.5	26	42	44	5.5	1905	(GN) Rail-motor
2a	LNW	240	17	25	36	81	11	1887	Precedent
b	LBS	042	20.7	28	38	78	16	1882	B
c	GW	440	20.6	36	56	80½	18	1903	City
d	NB	440	21.0	31	46	78	16	1876	476
3a	GC	440	26.5	42	61	81	20	1913	Director
b	LA	2/440	25.6	38	57	67	20	pre-1914	(Baldwin)
c	SR	3/440	28.3	42	67	79	25	1930	School
d	GW	2/440	20.6	38	59	80½	21	1904	County
4a	LY	442	26	35	59	87	17	1899	1400
b	GN	2/442	31	40	70	80	18	1902	251
c	CE	2/442	48	47	82	78	25	1914	(Baldwin)
d	GC	2/442	26.3	37	72	81	18	1903	8B
5a	LY	242T	18.8	40	67	68	25	1911	6
b	LNW	442T	22.4	40	75	75	19	1906	Precursor Tank
c	LNW	062T	17.0	34	44	53	16	1881	Coal Tank
d	LBS	2/462T	25.2	55	89	79½	21	1910	J
6a	LNW	060	15.0	29	29	62	14	1881	DX rebuilt
b	UP	2/060	30.2	66	66	51	28	pre-1914	(Baldwin)
c	SR	060	21.9	50	50	61	27	1938	Q
d	NE	060T	12.1	39	39	49	17	1898	E1
7a	SR	3/260	25.0	54	64	72	26	1928	U1
b	IS	260	26.4	44	55	73	25	1909	(Berlin Machine Co.)
c	SP	2/260	49.5	68	80	63	34	pre-1914	(Baldwin)
d	LNW	460	25.0	47	66	75	22	1911	*Prince*
8a	GW	2/460	27.1	55	72	80½	25	1903	*Lady*
b	LSW	4/460	31.5	55	77	79	22	1911	T14
c	LMS	4/460	30.5	60	80	81	25	1930	Claughton
9a	P	2/462	70	96	152	80	45	1914	K4s
b	GW	4/462	41.5	60	98	80½	28	1908	*The Great Bear*

Table 1 continued (locomotives not illustrated)

Ref.	Rail way	Wheel arr'g't	Grate Area (sq ft)	Weight (tons.) Adh.	Tot.	Wheel diameter (in.)	Nominal Tractive Effort (1000 lb.)	Date of first	Class or Builder
c	GN	3/462	41.3	60	92	80	30	1922	A1
d	LMS	4/462	50	67	108	81	40	1937	*Coronation*
10a	LMS	2/264T	26.7	52	88	69	25	1936	Stanier
b	N	4C/464	46	54	102	80	42	1910	Experimental
c	NY	2/464	82	87	160	79	43	1937	J-3a
d	LNE	4C/464	45	62	104	80	50	1929	10000
11a	LNW	080	20.5	49	49	53	24	1892	LNW
b	CB	2/080	50	95	95	57	49	1914	(Baldwin)
c	GN	2/280	27	67	76	56	32	1913	456
d	LMS	084T	23.6	67	88	53	30	1923	380
12a	B	2/282	70	99	127	64	55	pre-1914	(Baldwin)
b	PM	2/284	90	134	198	69	70	1941	(Lima)
c	CM	2/484	106	117	203	74	71	1937	(Baldwin)
13a	SS	2C/0100	37	66	66	51	47	1909	(Borsig-Berlin)
b	BS	4/2100	54	88	98	57	60	1909	36
c	CQ	2/2102	88	135	169	60	72	pre-1914	(Baldwin)
d	M	2/0100T	29	84	84	53	44	1908	(Berlin Machine Co.)
14a	GU	4C/2880	78	188	201	63	168	1913	(Baldwin)
b	E	6C/28882	90	340	380	63	245	1914	(Baldwin)
c	P	4/4444	92	125	225	80	65	1945	T1
d	LNE	6/2882T	56	144	178	56	73	1925	Garratt banker
15a	WM	4/4664	119	180	269	69	96	1940	(Baldwin)
b	V	4/2666	135	221	336	67	111	1945	(Lima)
c	B	4/2884	118	217	281	64	115	1944	(Baldwin)
16a	A	4/462264	58	109	213	71	66	1936	Beyer-Garratt
b	PO	4C/480	40	76	108	71	56	1932	(Chapelon)
c	LNW	080	20.5	49	49	53	24	1892	As 11a
d	LMS	4/462	50	67	108	81	40	1937	As 9d

Table 1 continued (locomotives not illustrated)

Ref.	Rail-way	Wheel arr'g't	Grate Area (sq ft)	Weight (tons.) Adh.	Tot.	Wheel dia-meter (in.)	Nominal Tractive Effort (1000 lb.)	Date of first	Class or Builder
Z1	GW	422	20.8	18	49	92½	13	1894	Dean single
Z2	GN	2/422	17.8	17	45	97	13	1884	Stirling single
Z3	LNW	3C/2220	20.5	31	46	85	19	1889	Teutonic
Z4	NE	440	19.7	34	51	85	17	1892	M
Z5	GE	460	26.5	44	63	78	22	1911	1500
Z6	GW	4/460	29.4	59	80	80½	32	1923	Castle
Z7	LMS	4/462	45	68	105	78	40	1933	Princess
Z8	LNE	3/462	41.3	66	103	80	36	1935	A4†
Z9	LMS	2/264T	25.0	55	86	69	24	1927	Fowler
Z10	LMS	4/2662T	44.5	122	156	63	46	1927	Garratt
Z11	UR	2/0102	85	154	181	61	92	1936	(Baldwin)
Z12	P	4/4464	122	175	276	69	102	1944	Q2
Z13	B	4C/0660	72	182	182	56	117	1903	2400
Z14	NP	4/2884	182	248	320	63	146	1929	5000
Z15	UP	4/4884	150	241	345	68	135	1941	4000
Z16	V	4C/210102	109	286	306	56	260	1918	800
Z17	SR	2/460	30	60	82	79	26	1925	King Arthur

† Streamlined

TABLE 2

Record Runs in Race to Scotland 1895

EAST COAST ROUTE, 21-22 AUGUST   LOAD 101 TONS

Distance* (miles)	Place	Time* (minutes)	Speed* (mph)	Engine No.	Class			Driver
—	King's Cross							
105.5	Grantham	101	62.7	668	GN	2/4–2–2		Falkinder
82.7	York	76	65.3	775	,,	,,		?
80.3	Newcastle	79	61.0	1621	NE	Class M1 4–4–0		Turner
124.4	Edinburgh	113	66.3	1620	,,	,, ,,		Nicholson
59.3	Dundee	57	62.5	293	NB	Class M 4–4–0		?
71.2	Aberdeen	78	54.8	262	,,	,, ,,		?

523.4		504	62.3	excluding time at rest
Total time 5 stops		16		
		520	60.4	from King's Cross to Aberdeen

WEST COAST ROUTE, 22-23 AUGUST   LOAD 73 TONS

Distance* (miles)	Place	Time* (mintes)	Speed* (mph)	Engine No.	Class			Driver
—	Euston							
158.1	Crewe	148	64.1	1309	LNW	3C/2–2–2–0		Walker
141.0	Carlisle	126	67.2	790	,,	Precedent 2–4–0		Robins
150.8	Perth	149.5	60.5	90	CR	Drummond 4–4–0		Crookson
89.7	Aberdeen	80.5	66.8	17	,,	Lambie 4–4–0		Soutar

539.6		504	64.2	excluding time at rest
Total time 3 stops		8		
		512	63.2	from Euston to Aberdeen

* From preceding place.

TABLE 3

Some record runs by British steam in the Twentieth Century

Run	1	2	3	4	5	6	7
Railway	GW	GW	GW	SR	LNE	LMS	LMS
Date	9.5.04	6.6.32	6.6.32	pre 1935	27.9.35	17.11.36	29.6.37
Engine No.	3065	5006	5005	777	2509†	6201	6220†
Class	4–2–2	Castle	Castle	K.Arthur	A4	Princess	*Coronation*
Ref.	Z1	Z6	Z6	Z17	Z8	Z7	89C
Load (ton)	120	195	210	345	230	260	270
S mph	71.3	81.7	77.3	69.2	82.8*	69.8	79.7
Miles	118.4	77.3	77.3	83.8	76.4	401.4	158.1
P mph	80.3	88.0	82.2	82.8	102	81.3	89
Miles	62.5	62.5	62.5	33.0	37.3	61.6	69.9
M mph	87	92	86	90	112	96	100

S mph was the average speed start-to-stop between the points named below
P mph   „   „   „   „   between the intermediate points named below.
M mph   „   „   momentary maximum speed

Run 1 S – Bristol to London (Paddington)	P – Shrivenham to Southall
Run 2 S – Swindon to Paddington	P – Shrivenham to Southall
Run 3 S – Paddington to Swindon	P – Southall to Shrivenham
Run 4 S – Salisbury to London (Waterloo)	P – Basingstoke to Esher
Run 5 S – King's Cross to Peterborough*	P – Hatfield to Mile-post 55
Run 6 S – Glasgow (Central) to London (Euston)	P – Weedon to Wembley
Run 7 S – Crewe to Euston	P – Welton to Willesden

† Streamlined. In these runs, only streamlined engines reached 100 mph.

* The train ran slowly through Peterborough in 55 min. 2 sec. from King's Cross.
The speed quoted corresponds to stopping at Peterborough in 55 mins. 17 sec.
as the train could easily have done, but Run 2 holds the British start-to-stop
record for steam.

Abbreviations of names of railways and railroads

A	Algerian
B	Baltimore & Ohio
BR	British Railways
BS	Belgian State
C	Caledonian
CB	Chicago Belt
CE	Chicago & Eastern Illinois
CM	Chicago, Milwaukee, St. Paul & Pacific
CQ	Chicago, Burlington & Quincy
E	Erie
GC	Great Central
GE	Great Eastern
GN	Great Northern
GU	Great Northern (USA)
GW	Great Western
IS	Italian State
LA	Louisiana & Arkansas
LBS	London, Brighton & South Coast
LMS	London, Midland & Scottish group (1923-48)
LNE	London & North Eastern group (1923-48)
LNW	London & North Western
LSW	London & South Western
LY	Lancashire & Yorkshire
M	Midi (France)
MR	Midland
N	Nord (France)
NB	North British
NE	North Eastern
NP	Northern Pacific
NY	New York Central
P	Pennsylvania
PM	Pere Marquette (USA)
PO	Paris–Orleans
SP	Southern Pacific
SR	Southern group (1923-48)
SS	Servian State
UP	Union Pacific
UR	Union
V	Virginian
WM	Western Maryland

INDEX

153